# AMERICA

## Too
## Good
## For
## Fascism

## Too
## Dumb
## For
## Democracy

Ian Gurvitz

ISBN 9798332871412

COVER IMAGE Shutterstock
COVER DESIGN Victoria Gapin

# TABLE OF CONTENTS

# FOREWORD

This is the fourth book I've written over the past decade centered on the rise, fall, and potential resurrection of Donald Trump.

From being mocked at the 2011 White House Correspondents' Dinner, to the 2015 escalator descent, through 3 elections, 2 impeachments, 88 felony indictments, 34 convictions, and a shooting, this dumb, deranged, deadly individual continues to dominate our political lives, and may have the power to destroy our way of life. This shouldn't be happening in the United States. Yet, it is.

This dangerous absurdity has reached the point that, every time I turn on the news, I'm reminded of an old joke about a guy who arrives in hell and is being shown around by a tour guide. They walk into a room where everyone's standing knee-deep in shit. The guy says, "Well, this doesn't seem so bad." Then an announcement booms over the loudspeakers: "Ok, break's over! Everybody back on their heads!"

# CHAPTER ONE


AMERICA

COME
FOR
THE
MYTH

STAY
FOR
THE
MADNESS

I was raised on the post-World War Two American myth. I came of age in the '60s American metamorphosis. Now I'm living through the 21st century American madness.

Once upon a time we were Captain America. We fought a revolution to free ourselves from tyranny. Battled our inner demons to keep the union together. Defeated European fascism. Twice. Sure, we had our ill-begotten, mission-creep misadventures -- Vietnam, Iraq, Afghanistan -- but always with the best of intentions. And, yes, we're the only country in history to drop an atomic bomb. Ok, two atomic bombs. Still, we managed to win the Cold War without dropping another one.

We're the good guys. The land of the free, and the home of the brave. The heart of western democracy. Sweet land of liberty. The shining city on the hill. A beacon of freedom, and refuge for the world's downtrodden, though that's often in comparison to whatever war-torn, anarchic narco-state they had the misfortune of being born into. America. It may not be paradise, but it beats the living shit out of getting kidnapped, raped, murdered by drug gangs, or starving to death. No one's risking his life to climb a wall to get _out_ of here. Well, not yet, anyway.

We're a nation of laws, crafted by the best of us to protect us from the worst of us, with the Constitution as our North Star, despite being subjected to the whims of whoever happens to be sitting on the Supreme Court at any given time. That stark reality is now more evident than ever.

Still, for all our virtues, America in theory has always been more noble than America in practice. We've had assassinations, attempted assassinations, bombings, police shootings, political scandals, riots, domestic terror attacks, rampant poverty, homelessness, income inequality, drugs, alcoholism, a world-shattering rate of incarceration in the prison-industrial complex, and a seemingly never-ending spree of mass murders, thanks to our malignant gun fetish. The U.S. has over four hundred million guns in circulation and more gun deaths per year than any "civilized" nation.

Oh, and slavery. Slavery is America's birth defect. Our imperfect founding fathers enshrined the ideal of personal freedom in the Constitution, based on the inherent value of each individual life. Unfortunately, they pulled up short on exactly which individual lives were entitled to it -- like only Caucasian, land-owning men. By definition, you shouldn't be able to limit an absolute right, but somehow they managed to square that circle, based on the flawed idea that one can calculate the value of a "whole person." For all their wisdom and foresight, they weren't able to think themselves out of their cultural zeitgeist.

We killed more than 600,000 of our own people over slavery. Defeated, the South rose again by way of The John Birch Society, the KKK, the DAR, the White Citizens Council, the America First Movement, Jim Crow, and neo-Nazis, along with an army of segregationist Dixiecrat politicians who shape-shifted into Republicans, then tried to fob themselves off as the party of Lincoln. If Lincoln came back from the dead and saw what was going on in his name, he'd blow his own head off.

In the effort to form a more perfect union, our better angels have been locked in a Jekyll and Hyde struggle with our inner demons. At times, those demons were pacified with national pastimes, from sports and alcohol to sex and drugs, or we rose above them in response to mutual injury, like during Pearl Harbor, or 9/11. But then they would flare up, and we'd be at each other's throats, like during the '60s Vietnam protests.

Raised on a Manichean, WWII mentality, some on the Right waved the flag in a "my country, right or wrong!" stance that equated dissent with disloyalty, oblivious to the idea that the right to protest is exactly what made the country worth fighting for. They didn't get that there is a fundamental difference between a form of government and a particular administration's policies. It lead to half the country defending an ill-begotten war, while the other half seemed to retreat into cynicism about the founding principles of the country itself.

Yet, somehow, we managed to fight it out without succumbing to yet another Civil War, and were able to cleanse ourselves by reclaiming who we were. Tacking back toward that North Star.

We had a national identity and a national purpose. We may have disagreed on the nature of that identity or the specifics of that purpose, but we didn't disagree on the goals, themselves, or the value of having goals, and unifying principles. Maybe it was all based on the illusion of unity, but who cares if it was the illusion that held us together. And even though there were fascists, racists, and other assorted megalomaniacs who made inroads in politics, including mayors, state representatives, governors, and members of Congress, they were ultimately seen as aberrations. Crackpots. Throwbacks standing athwart history, yelling "Stop!" And we eventually purged them from the system. Despite our internal struggles, American democracy always seemed safely tied to the dock of reason, sanity, and patriotism

But that was back in The Before Times. After centuries of battling for the heart, mind and soul of the country, we've officially cracked, and are on the verge of a national psychotic breakdown, with one side living in a world of principles, the other living in a world of power.

What's the line about America and England? Two countries separated by a common language. That's us: One country, two different realities. The American myth has dissolved into the American madness, and a dangerous flirtation with fascism -- the one thing democracy was designed to be a bulwark against. Our differences are not just geographical, but social, economic, generational, intellectual, cultural, emotional, and psychological. And our politics has devolved into a zero sum game. There's no *E Pluribus Unum*. We're not even a house divided against itself. There is no house. There is no self.

We've become a country in which a crazed, hateful, delusional, power-mad, self-righteous, theocratic bomb-throwing radical anti-government insurrectionist minority refers to itself as conservative. Where truth isn't truth. Where freedom is license. Anarchy is order. Fascists are patriots. And religious moralists are bigots and closet perverts. Where doctors are demonized, compassion is weakness, knowledge is suspect, and education is scorned. And all it took to stoke our weaknesses was a cartoonish, orange-faced, reality show carnival barker with the brains of a hamster and the morals of a mob boss.

Watching this country fracture makes me think of Robert Oppenheimer staring at the exploding A-bomb and intoning a line from the Bhagavad Gita: "I am become death; the destroyer of worlds."

But, how the fuck did we get here? How did we manage to find the worst person in the country and give him the most important job on the planet? How did we allow a dumb, racist criminal, and reality show clown get his tiny, sweaty, rapey hands on executive power, sell us out to a sworn enemy, lie about a fatal disease, steal documents, attack the government in a treasonous attempt to overturn an election, get hit with 88 felony indictments, and (so far) 34 convictions, brag about wanting to be a dictator, and still have a shot at doing it all over again? If someone broke into your house and attacked your family, would you toss him a key and say, "Hey, come back tomorrow! You haven't met the dog!"

Trump is a Frankenstein monster created out of the worst parts of America. The worship of money and fame, tabloid journalism, reality television, social media, a cable news addiction to shiny, noisy objects, fear of change, red state resentment, and a vulnerability to conspiracy theories, propaganda, and disinformation.

He's someone who fobbed himself off as intelligent to cover his bone-deep stupidity. Someone who resented being looked down on by the upper class folks whose ranks he was trying to claw his way into. Someone who could stir up hate because he felt hate. Someone who could whip up a crowd by playing off their petty grievances because he was petty and aggrieved.

He is a homegrown Hitler fetishist whose every move has been cribbed from the Mein Kampf playbook. A one-man goose-stepping Nazi tribute band. Trump is Hitler 2.0. Or, as I referred to him in an earlier book: Hitler Lite. All the flavor, with 10% less hate.

Donald Trump didn't create our present nightmare. But he was the catalyst for it. A single 2015 escalator ride launched us into the hell-scape of the American psyche, as a dumb, racist, venal, crooked, grotesque, life-long criminal, pathological liar and professional mind-fucker pussy grabbed national attention, and presidential power. And now, after nine years of this insanity, he has a credible chance of clawing his way back. Despite his many crimes, and convictions, his popularity among the die-hard faithful seems unshakable. And the attempt on his life only solidified his supporters' Christ-like devotion. That's not on him. That's on us. He didn't destroy us. He revealed us.

Trump didn't elect himself. When he proclaimed: "When Mexico sends their people, they're not sending their best. They're bringing drugs, they're bringing crime, they're rapists…" the response from an intelligent, civilized, educated public should have been: "Get the fuck outta here." He should have been laughed off the national stage.

Instead, in 2016, he got 63 million votes. Then, despite trying to kill the Affordable Care Act, being accused of sexual assault, statutory rape, extorting a foreign leader to interfere in an American election, the Mueller investigation, Helsinki, Charlottesville, Lafayette Square, the first of two impeachments, lying about Covid, resulting in hundreds of thousands of preventable deaths, and an economic collapse. After all that, he got 74 million votes. Yes, there was higher turnout in 2020. Still, at that point, we should have completely rejected him. We didn't.

And, now they're ready to vote for him again, despite attacking Congress and trying to assassinate his Vice President in order to overturn an election. Despite proclaiming his intention to become our first home-grown dictator and get revenge on his enemies. How did "Give me liberty or give me death" become "Change the election results or I'll get my people to smash a cop in the head with a fire extinguisher and take a dump in the Capitol?" "I regret that I have but one shit to give for my country!"

People died. Thousands were arrested, convicted, and incarcerated. And he did it all in broad daylight. In public. His *mens rea* has always been painfully obvious. He wanted to retain power and stay out of prison. Call it insurrection if that's the legal term. But he didn't "incite an insurrection." He launched an attack. It was one thing. One plot. And it was treason.

Trump re-awakened the lingering virus of hate in this country, preying on our worst instincts and cultural divides. It's ironic that one of his early slogans was "Drain the Swamp." In fact, Trump is a creature of the American swamp. He didn't create it. He oozed out of it.

One might think that, simply by virtue of living in a country founded on the principles of equality and basic human dignity, and governed by justice, and equal protection under the law, that America would manufacture better people. We haven't. Something's gone wrong in the American factory because we've mass produced too many defective Americans and, like extras in *The Walking Dead*, these mutants now walk amongst us, waving signs, ranting on social media, voting Republican, and eating everything in sight except, sadly, brains.

Despite being home to the greatest universities in the world, we are possessed of a venal, bone-deep stupidity, combined with an unhinged anger, raging insecurity, class resentment and the primal need to punish someone else for our own misfortunes. Trump is the champion of their grievances.

His people think he is their voice, but he looks down on them with all the disdain of a sadistic little bastard pouring boiling water on an anthill. He despises the system, as his supporters do. But for different reasons. They think it keeps them from succeeding in it. He knows it keeps him from looting it.

Still, just as when he first inflicted himself on our lives, it all leads back to a single, fundamental question: Why? Why would anyone vote for this dumb, deranged, dangerous, diabolical clown? When did American exceptionalism devolve into American special needs?

Trump is the idiots' avatar. He struts onstage, fat tiny thumbs in the air, shit-eating grin on his face as he lumbers into his patented "double masturbation dance" and people cheer. He claims he's being indicted "for them" and they cheer. He claims the government is after them and they're going through Trump. And they cheer. He claims to be their voice and their retribution and they cheer. He even gets shot (or maybe just shot at) and raises his fist, yelling, "Fight!" and they cheer. They're empowered by his defiance. His badass, anarchic energy. They might as well be at a Death Metal concert, flashing devil horns.

MAGA is rooted in class resentment. Racism. Fear of change. Fear of being culturally displaced. It's always been here, occasionally lying dormant. But all it took to activate it was Barack Obama's election. This caused a right wing freak-out, which manifested itself in the Tea Party, which morphed into the Town Hall protesters, the Freedom Caucus and then MAGA. I referred to it as angry, White America's last gasp. Turns out it wasn't. It was its reanimating breath of life.

But there's more going on here than just political affiliation. It's near religious devotion. Like most sane adults, I mocked the ludicrous Trump imagery. The virile, defiant Trump/Jesus being nailed to the cross while being poked with sharp sticks by Nancy Pelosi. Trump as Superman. Trump as Rambo, with six-pack abs, gripping an automatic weapon. Trump as a Top Gun fighter pilot. Trump as George Washington, proudly sitting tall on his white horse. Even though in reality he is 350 pounds of rancid Mac 'n' Cheese in a dumpy suit and dick-compensator tie, his face spackled with orange goop and his idiotic hair whipped up into an Aqua-netted, soft-serve, tornado coiffure.

The Trump art isn't representational. It's devotional. The imagery isn't about depicting him as he is. It's about capturing how he makes them feel. It expresses the depth of their emotional need and pathetic but no less dangerous devotion.

But his wretched refuse are not the sum total of the movement. They are and always have been a shadow play. Misdirection from the real, more ominous MAGA threat. As Michael Corleone said in Godfather III -- an unfortunately flawed sequel featuring some major league scenery chewing, but one from which there are a handful of quotable lines: "Our true enemy has yet to show his face."

# CHAPTER TWO

# MAGA
# IS
# A
# MULTI-HEADED
# MONSTER

In previous books I chalked up the extreme MAGA phenomenon to the red states. The Great Pacific Garbage Patch of America. America's wretched refuse. A free-floating barge of beer, cotton candy, spilled soda, chili cheese fries, stale popcorn, dog piss, and sawdust. Or whatever that stanky shit is on the ground after a carney packs up and leaves town. The MAGATs who plastered their trailers, trucks and boats with Trump flags and snarky juvenile bumper stickers about owning the libtards, mindlessly following each other like circus elephants clinging to each other's tails. Trump's flying monkeys. His mutant army of horn-wearing, bear-spraying, cop-killing mutants. The missing teeth, beer-guzzling, book-burning, tatted-up redneck trailer trash. God-fearing, slack-jawed, mullet-headed, knuckle-dragging mouth-breathers. Dumb, angry, delusional, malevolent, insecure, brainwashed, violent, racist shitheads. Dumbfucks, sex abusers, wife beaters, cousin-fuckers, pussy grabbers, gun freaks, Jesus freaks and Jesus grifters. Pasty, self-loathing, pray-the-gay-away closet cases and fetus-loving Christo-fascists. Bellicose, self-proclaimed alpha males and steroidal, freedumb-fighting weekend warrior beer-gutted cos-players, armed to their rotting teeth with AR-15s, lumbering around the woods playing minuteman while blasting away at beer cans. Paranoid, Kool-Aid drinking, video game-addicted incels. Shmucks, cucks, perverts, dopes, morons, and dropouts. Election deniers, Qanon Qrackheads, CTE victims, sexual deviants. Inbreds, meth-heads, hags, slags, twits, shits, half-wits, drunks, skunks, and creepy little punks. Fox-watching, Viking-horned, grunting, low-rent, oil-slicked swamp rats. Survivalists with bomb shelters, and shelves stacked with condoms, beer, Spam, and automatic weapons for when the government or the zombies come for their shit. The red hat, rake and pitchfork crowd who attacked the Capitol on January 6th, along with their sister wives, cousin girlfriends, and baby mamas. The clandestine internet warriors on a myriad of dark, deranged platforms, blasting away with their angry little trigger fingers. The ones to whom Trump said, "I am your voice." "I am your warrior. I am your justice. I am your retribution." People who think God and guns go together like grits and gravy, giving them divine sanction for their hatred. Lonesome losers who fell through the cracks of society. Capitalism's also-rans. The lumpy proletariat. Basement-dwelling Willie Lomans demanding that "attention must be paid!" These are America's truck nuts.

But the fallacy was in mistaking the shock troops for the real MAGA. I first saw Trump as a menace to society. What I missed was that the menace <u>was</u> society. The dark forces in the country that have always manipulated American life found a powerful spokesperson and/or useful idiot in Donald Trump. MAGA is, and they'll probably hate the use of this word: diverse. It's all the forces in the country who think America belongs to them, and only them.

They are Shadow MAGA. Powerful corporations, rogue billionaires, crazed, evangelical Christo-fascists whether motivated by greed, or some twisted, moralistic, rapture-based prosperity gospel perversion of religion. As declared in the Heritage Foundation's Project 2025, their goal is to hit the brakes on the social revolution that took hold with the New Deal, worked itself through the Great Society and the '60s liberation movements, and slam America into reverse, back to the 1950s, then blast back to the 1850s, then surge into hyper-space back to some mythical, Jesus-riding-a-dinosaur Biblical Stone Age.

It's tight-ass, pasty white, evangelical Moral Majority-types, hiding behind freedom-loving patriotic monikers like "Americans for an American America," "Moms For Chastity, or "MILFs For Liberty."

It's corporations. Tech billionaires. Hypocritical politicians whose public personas are masks for their private activities. Soulless, liver-spotted country club types and 19th hole alcoholics. Jowly, man-titted Republicans with pink polo shirts and blazers sucking down 18-year-old Scotch, while bemoaning the shoddy condition of the putting greens. People for whom America was, and always should be, a restricted country club.

From old school moguls to new age tech bros. They own things, like the means of production, and Supreme Court judges. People who see government as a system to be gamed, laws things to be flouted or circumvented, and politicians things to be bribed or threatened. They have the attitude of organized crime but the cover of respectable society. People for whom democracy isn't as much a system of government based on the will of the people, as a smokescreen. Misdirection in a magic act. Something for the little people to live by. People for whom the Constitution may as well have been written on an Etch A Sketch.

Change has never come easy in America. Whether it was social, financial, or regulatory, there have always been forces batting against it. Medicare. Medicaid. Social Security. Civil rights. Money for public education. Unions. Higher minimum wage. Seat belts. Warnings on cigarettes. Women's right to vote. Women's health care. Worker safety. Workers' comp. Affirmative action. Affordable health care. LGBTQ rights. Any attempt to improve the quality of life, protect people from misfortune, or right an historical wrong has been met with a tidal wave of forces battling against it, whether they carried guns, Bibles, or briefcases.

Whether it's based in fear, lack of empathy, or just down and dirty greed, misanthropy, or love of power. They have always been here, but they've never been so emboldened. And so organized. They have private agendas, yet, at times, the Venn diagram of their forces is almost a perfect circle. They are the real axis of evil.

## CORPORATE MONEY MAGA

Henry Ford invented automotive mass production, and created an iconic American company. He built the Model T, the T-bird, and the Mustang. He also hired thugs to bust unions, and hated Jews, though I'm not sure whether that was for fun or profit. He's just one of the corporate titans who got rich off the capitalism part of the American dream while battling the democratic part of it. They may have created and manufactured products that made people's lives better, but mankind was not always their concern.

Carnegie. Mellon. Colt. Whitney. Frick. Hughes. Kennedy. Morgan. Vanderbilt. Rockefeller. Getty. Gould. Edison. Duke. Walton. There are the names you know and the names you don't. They owned the means of production and put America to work. They created iconic American companies, built skyscrapers, bridges, and railroads, and provided the products and creature comforts we now consider our birthright. They also fought unionization, engaged in price fixing, bribery, blackmail, battled government regulations, meddled in politics, or turned a blind eye to selling products that were unsafe, whether physically or mentally addicting, and then warped our minds with advertising to make us think we not only wanted, but needed them.

They invented. They innovated. They dominated. Occasionally they corrupted. They also used the system to game the system, employing money and power to fight regulation, even to the point of branding the idea of regulation as an un-American crime against the invisible, divine hand of the market. Then, like crime scene cleaners, many acid-washed their reputations by slapping their names on museums, hospitals, universities, charities, foundations, scholarships, libraries, and concert halls.

Nineteenth century moguls eventually gave way to 20th and 21st century titans. Sackler. Zuckerberg. Gates. Thiel. Adelson. Wynn. Musk. (Yes, we actually grew our own Bond

Villain.) The Koch Brothers, (Or brother, now that one of them is dead. I can't remember which one and I'm too lazy to Google it. I mean, in the grand scheme of things, does it really matter?) The Mercers. Murdochs. The late Sheldon Adelson. Melted-face casino mogul Steve Wynn. The Hobby Lobby guy. The Home Depot guy. Hedge fund managers. Tech entrepreneurs. Casino owners. Media moguls. Social media giants. Brokerage kings. Crypto kings. Wrestling CEOS. Bankers. Oil billionaires. Sports team CEOs.

Corporate money MAGA has always been there. It was car companies fighting mandatory seatbelts. Cigarette companies stonewalling warning labels on their products, while swearing before Congress that nicotine wasn't addictive. Gun manufacturers and the NRA battling any attempts to regulate their products, leading to the daily American carnage, where body counts and murder rates are rattled off like sports scores. (I assume they had killing off their consumer base built into their business model, and that it made more bottom line sense to accept a level of customer turnover than make their products less harmful. Or go into another business.)

MAGA is the pharmaceutical industry fighting lower drug prices and the health insurance industry fighting Medicare for all, branding it as "socialized medicine" that will lead to government death panels. (We already have death panels. They're called actuarial tables.) MAGA is crazed evangelicals suing over their rights not to be forced to bake gay wedding cakes. It's the oil and gas industry ignoring rising CO2 levels, sea levels, and more volatile weather patterns, while raging against clean energy. President Carter put solar panels on the roof of the White House. Ronald Reagan smugly, arrogantly and ceremoniously took them down. As a former president and relative of an MIT scientist declared: "Climate change is bullshit. It's a Democrat hoax." (I yearn for the day when Mar-a-Lago is under six feet of water and him along with it.)

Once upon a time corporations wielded power by

invading Washington with lobbyists, bribes, and hookers. Then Citizens United changed the game. As the whitest man in politics, Mitt Romney, proclaimed, "Corporations are people, my friends." No. Thanks to Citizens United, corporations are the new people. They own the means of production, the means of communication, and occasionally the means of legislation. Citizens United made it possible for shadow organizations, under the guise of advocating for a point of view, to give unlimited dark money dollars to political action committees while pretending not to coordinate with a particular campaign.

Dark money spending rose from under $5 million in 2006, to almost $1 billion in 2022. And that's coming from around 465 billionaires. Many big money donors will often give to both parties, hedging their bets. You may want one side to win. But you may still need the other side to give you what you want.

Corporate America is already hedging their bets, and doubling down on MAGA. Even in early 2024 the moguls at the Davos summit were gaming out the election, ready to show Trump the love he'll demand for fear that he'll fuck with their profits. But even if they get their tax breaks, perhaps those corporate types should consider what Putin has done with wealthy business owners when he suddenly thinks he should have a share of, or all of, their companies.

## POLITICAL MAGA.

In 2009, former SNL writer and performer, Al Franken prevailed in a narrow run-off election in Minnesota and took his seat in the United States Senate. At the time Senator James Inhofe (R-OK; recently deceased) cracked, "Looks like we're getting the clown." My comment at the time was if "clowns in the Senate was the subject, then Franken had some pretty big shoes to fill."

This was the same Senator Inhofe who stood on the Senate floor and held a snowball in his hand as a way of demonstrating that since water can freeze, "global warming" wasn't real. This dangerously childish level of belief, or cold, dark cynicism has infected our politics. Whether he was a shill for the fossil fuel industry or a religious zealot, who knows. Maybe both. You almost have to admire the balls it took to assume the public is just that dumb.

The stereotype of the Washington politician has always been some mash-up of the glad-handing, backslapping pandering, marginally corrupt, bombastic, hypocritical, lying power-hungry poseur who prefers the appearance of doing something to the actual doing of it. The Foghorn Leghorn phony who grandstands on the Senate floor, like Ted Cruz -- the bastard child of Satan and Ed Grimley --  doing his 21-hour anti-Obamacare filibuster by reading *Green Eggs and Ham*, which was before he bugged out to Cancun when the power went out in Texas and his constituents were freezing to death.

Even those dedicated public servants who fought to improve the lives of Americans weren't necessarily without flaws. Some lead complicated lives, battled inner demons, but still managed to come out on the right side of history. But don't look to elected officials for moral leadership. Be happy if they can pull off political leadership.

I imagine some old school conservatives actually believed their rhetoric, and lived decent, moral lives, while others postured about honesty in public while hooking up with Senate pages in private. They said what they needed to say. Then did what they wanted to do. And if they got busted they often lost their seats either by resigning or in the next election, and eventually transitioned into lobbyists. But that was at a time when hypocrisy was still a thing.

Not that we didn't have the occasional megalomaniac who perverted our lives for power, ushering in a wave of mass psychosis, like during the '50s Army McCarthy hearings. McCarthy rode the red scare anti-communist paranoia of the day to advance his own agenda, whether it was ambition, greed, or making sure he never ran out of alcohol. He set a new low bar for working a lie for his own benefit, while destroying the lives of many innocent people as his influence ranged from D.C. to Hollywood.

But even the usual opportunists working the system to get their hands on power were ultimately not bomb throwers hell-bent on taking down the entire system. Even if they made bomb-thrower noises, they ultimately accepted the will of the majority.

They could compromise to pass laws and avert disasters if either there was sufficient horse-trading, or their arms or testicles were successfully twisted. As LBJ famously stated: "If you've got 'em by the balls, their hearts and minds will follow." They knew the value of quid pro quo. When they gained a foothold on power they eventually lapsed back into business as usual.

But we've now crossed a line. The mutant strain of the GOP has now become dominant. The bomb throwers have gotten hold of political power and are doing their worst, combining political opportunism, zealotry and stupidity with a heavy dose of Jesus.

We've entered a brave, and dangerous new world. Even old-timey Republican stalwarts like McConnell, McCarthy, Grassley, Graham, Thune, Romney, Rubio, and Marsha Blackburn, who looks and sounds like she just jump started her vibrator with a truck battery, have made their Faustian bargain and are playing along with the MAGATs, as a way of keeping their seats or blasting their way through an election without a primary challenge. If it was ever about principles, it's not anymore. It's about power. One hundred and forty-seven Republicans voted against certifying the results of the 2020 election.

MAGA has officially planted its freak flag in Congress. MTG, the three-toed Georgia Mrs. Potato Head, treats the House of Representatives like it's hillbilly performance art. There's Bobo from Colorado, who should raise campaign funds by offering to let $25 dollar donors feel her up in a theater, $50 for a reach around. They are slutty Betty and Veronica. There's Missouri's own scampering, raised-fisted little pony, Josh Hawley. Ohio's J.D. Vance, a guy with the nasty smugness of an old west gambler who keeps a derringer in his boot, who has now been chosen as Trump's VP. There's Gosar, Cruz, Jordan, Gaetz, Biggs, Comer, Tuberville. And, perhaps in an effort to make Tuberville look senatorial by comparison there's his newly minted Alabama colleague Katie Britt whose deranged, near-hysterical response to the 2024 State of the Union address arrived with the satire baked in, like dried apricots in a Christmas fruitcake.

We reached the full Kardashianization of politics with erstwhile Congressman George Santos – a mash-up of gay MAGA and grifter MAGA who took Trump-style bullshit to performance art levels. Satan's version of drag queen story hour.

They even elected a self-proclaimed Jesus freak as Speaker of the House, who claims that his political ideas are all in the Bible and that the Lord personally told him to become Moses. Given their literal interpretation of all things Biblical one only wishes he'd grab his staff and walk into the sea.

And those are just the ones who made it to the show. There are also the lunatics who couldn't break out of the minors but are far from giving up the grift. Kari Lake. The Norma Desmond of Arizona, who denied her election loss and is now making a run for the Senate, having proven herself even too crazy for Trump's VP pick. There's spawn of Oprah, Dr. Oz, who carpetbagged his way from Jersey and made a run for a Pennsylvania Senate seat, using the millions he made hawking vitamin supplements. The fact that his Democratic opponent John Fetterman had a stroke during the election tightened that race way too much for comfort. Georgia ran a block of wood for Senate in Herschel Walker. It's not merely that he was dumb and "somehow" got through college so he could play football. It's that he was dumb and obviously brain damaged. Sure, he could take a hand-off and blast his way through a defensive line and race into the end zone but Walker wasn't even capable of taking a pronoun and finding his way to the end of a sentence.

And there are still the state and local MAGATs running for local office while making flirty eyes with Washington. Texas Governor Greg Abbott, the Dr. Strangelove of Lone Star politics. His Hank Hill Lt. Gov., Dan Patrick. Seemingly ever-crooked AG Ken Paxton. Florida's Ron DeSantis, who, when he tries to force a smile sports the same pained expression as a 6-month old who just blasted out his diaper.

MAGA isn't only playing in the majors. They're cagey enough to play small ball, running for state government, school boards and city council seats so they can influence local policy, like banning books and blocking the teaching of slavery. Like entrepreneurial little cancer cells they're determined to infect every part of the body politic.

# LEGAL MAGA

The Federalist Society may brand itself as an organization dedicated to individual liberty, traditional values and the rules of law, but that's just a mask for a political agenda that uses the legal system to slam the brakes on social progress

They use the system to game the system, along with their constitutional " originalist" rhetoric to promote a right wing political agenda, while anyone who advances a different agenda is called an "activist." Theoretically, if "originalist" was actually a thing, we wouldn't need a Supreme Court to interpret the Constitution or write opinions. We could just run it through ChatGPT and it would spit out whether a particular law was or wasn't constitutional.

Six out of nine Supreme Court judges are Federalist Society members. Ninety percent of the judges appointed by Trump were also members. John Eastman, who looks like the Gestapo agent who got his face melted at the end of *Raiders of the Lost Ark*, right down to the fedora and trench coat, is a member. Eastman was the author of the memo that provided the strategy for January 6th, and was one of the speakers on that stage. Also along for the treason ride was Jeffrey Clark, who made a power move to replace then acting AG Jeffrey Rosen, until he was threatened with mass resignations. Another member is Trump lawyer Kenneth Chesebro, who was indicted in Wisconsin over the fake elector scheme to subvert the 2020 election.

The Federalist Society also gifted us numerous federal and state judges, including Judge Aileen Cannon, who, despite the claustrophobic confines of working inside Trump's pocket, made sure to slow walk the Florida documents trial into oblivion. At first, her rulings on Trump motions were clever enough to avoid accusations of corruption and being replaced, while kicking the can down the road and postponing any chance of a trial until after the election. Then she just dropped the pretense and tossed it out.

And as nefarious as their efforts have been, they have recently been turbocharged with a massive donation, courtesy of Barre Seid, a 92-year-old manufacturing magnate, known for his contributions to right wing causes like fighting against action on climate change. But his most recent play was gifting $1.6 billion to the Federalist Society. Nothing like reaching your 90s and making sure your legacy is to fuck up life for everyone who comes after you.

Then there's Clarence Thomas, who launched his Supreme Court career via a pubic hair on a Coke can and graduated to several decades on the bench and now seems virtually owned by a Nazi memorabilia collector. Despite his wife's actions on January 6th, Clarence still refuses to recuse himself from any Trump-related case. Does anyone really believe that in the heat of January 2021, while Trump was lying about the election being stolen, then losing over 60 lawsuits, meeting with phony slates of electors, arm-twisting Secretaries of State and governors, organizing the "Stop the Steal" rally, threatening the life of his vice president, compiling a war room at the Willard Hotel, and then sending his people to attack the Capitol, that the events of the day never came up at the Thomas dinner table?

Our system of justice is hanging by a thread as daily rulings filter down from the Supreme Court, which, in early March, agreed to take the Trump immunity case. And then in July, they exceeded all crooked expectations by granting Trump virtual immunity from all crimes, past, present, and future while punting that trial into oblivion. This decision removed any pretense of legitimate constitutional interpretation. The six person majority should not only wear black robes, but black hoods as well, as they have set themselves up as grand high legal executioners.

It's the ultimate in 21st century American mindfucking to use the system to game the system and ultimately subvert the system while preserving the illusion that there still is a system.

## MEDIA MAGA.

Fuck off, Rupert Murdoch. Fuck all the way off and die, you vile, greedy, cynical, power-hungry, money–grubbing, wrinkled, withered, gnarly, Emperor Palpatine look-alike motherfucker. You couldn't stay down under and fuck up your own country? You had to come up here and attack us? Was the money worth the misery you caused? No one went down to your tropical paradise and peddled bullshit for money. We left you alone with your beaches, opera houses, kangaroos, mamba snakes, dingos, and no-helmet football. Australians always seem like nice, friendly people, but I guess those penal colony genes slipped through.

Launched in 1996, Fox News is a disinformation Death Star. A bolt gun firing lies directly into the brains of red state Americans, poisoning the American conversation, while perverting our concept of news and truth.

Fox was crafted and shaped by the late sexual abuser and Nixon media guru Roger Ailes, pushed by aggro thugs like Bill O'Reilly, and Sean Hannity, then guided into the 21st century by cadres of blond bimbettes from Gretchen Carlson, and Megyn Kelly to Laura Ingraham, Tomi Lahren, and (non-blond) Judge Winebox. (Ingraham is the second runner up to Kellyanne Conway in the Miss Hatchet Face USA contest.) They are right wing show ponies, saying hateful shit for money. Spitting lies for attention. And possibly working out daddy issues.

Then there's Tucker Carlson, and Jesse Watters, each sporting a face so punchable it should be a carnival game where if you can smack the cocky smirk off it you win a stuffed bear. Carlson was the "it" boy for years until he fell out of favor, and is now about to do a show for Russian Television. At some point, they just drop the pretense and come out.

Murdoch unleashed America's demons by burrowing into its lizard brain, creating a disinformation fear and hate loop and angry counter reality. Sophistry meets philosophical relativism meets freedom of speech, and the American tradition of valuing all points of view morphed into the whitewashing of information and the mainstreaming of lies. Hate speech spewed under the guise of free speech. "We distort, contort, and incite. You obey." This was Goebbels-style mind-bending, combined with Russian-style disinformation, devoured by people without the skepticism to question something coming out of the TV, especially when it fed their victim narrative. Every day an assortment of angry thugs, perky blonds, and soft, manicured metrosexuals conspires to distort truth and sell their viewers on the idea that their misery is some smarty pants liberal's fault, while throwing in a dash of schlocky patriotism and religious persecution. Lie. Rinse. Repeat.

The $787 million Dominion judgment against Fox should have served as a teachable moment, even if the lesson is not wanting to be sued for almost a billion dollars. Still, they may have dumped Tucker but they'll never abandon the brand.

Not that America didn't have a rich tradition of right wing radio. There was Father Coughlin, who had tens of millions of listeners in the 1930s. He insisted that democracy was doomed and that our choices were fascism or communism. He chose fascism. We even had our pre-Trump, famous anti-Semitic isolationist in Charles Lindbergh.

Though not that all conservative media was propaganda. William F. Buckley launched *The National Review* and *Firing Line*, during the 1960s. A hyper intelligent champion for old school values at best, a blue-blooded, over-privileged warrior against social change at worst. Buckley actually did have the best words, and joyfully flaunted them. But at least there was substance and a belief system underneath it. Buckley had a searing intelligence, albeit tinged with a *soupcon* of Park Avenue elitism and cultural arrogance. He was a great mind and an eloquent advocate for his worldview, whether or not you agreed with it.

We also had our own cadres of conservative authors,

publishers, and pundits. Ivy league-educated men in suits and pocket hankies who sported class privilege along with the illusion that they could rock a bowtie. George Will, for one.

(Note: Bowties are a uniquely ridiculous style of neckwear. If you're over the age of five and are standing in front of a mirror, clipping on, or horror of horrors, tying your own bowtie, you have a completely misplaced sense of style along with a dangerously inflated sense of your own cultural superiority.)

Then there was Rush. Rush Limbaugh launched his show in 1988 and was nationally syndicated until his long-awaited death in 2021. A one-man assault weapon against a changing American society, Limbaugh's avid listeners referred to themselves as "dittoheads," avid fanboys and who'd call in to echo his every word and lavish praise and near worship on the host. Limbaugh's audience was estimated at over 15 million listeners.

For those who prefer a little kink with their crazy, there's always Milo Yiannopoulos, or the OG bomb thrower, Ann Coulter. With her trademark smirk and long, flowing mane, Coulter is like an Afghan hound strutting leash-less at the Westminster Dog show but instead of prancing around the ring she jumps up in the crowd and pisses on the judges or humps some hairy little Shih Tzu. Coulter is now on the anti-Trump train for some Republican fever dream he didn't deliver for her.

Right wing media has gone from expressing a point of view to creating an alternate, counter-factual reality. The old guard gave way to a new wave of media monsters. From Tucker Carlson's childish sneer to the rhythmic flapping of Ben Shapiro's 100-legged eyebrows. It's like his face is at war with itself. Fox may be the OG of hate TV news but they wove a spider web of hate sites.

OANN, Newsmax. Sinclair. 4CHAN. The Daily Caller. Alex Jones. Hate media with a side of snake oil. Politics and the grift not just working side by side but synergistically. Armed insurrection fueled by revolution and vitamin supplements.

For those who are MAGA-curious, or perversely pride themselves on being independent thinkers by ignoring facts and embracing crackpot conspiracy theories, there's former stand-up comic, bug-eating show host, and Colonel Kurtz look-alike Joe Rogan, who in early February signed a new deal with Sirius radio for $250 million. And in the weirdest twist of the 21$^{st}$ century great upside-down, a demented Bond villain has taken over the most powerful platform for information and communication in X/Twitter.

We Americans are easily amused. We love the clown shows. It works in Rock 'n' Roll, and in the WWE, and now in what we nostalgically call "the news." CNN, in the race for cable news eyeballs, is tacking right in what seems to be little more than a calculated business decision to scrape off some of that Fox audience. Even MSNBC monetarily hired former RNC chairman Ronna (Romney) McDaniel until an uproar among viewers caused them to un-hire her.

Peddling anger for eyeballs, the right wing infotainment complex has successfully battled truth to a draw, creating not only counter-narratives, but a counter-reality. It's bread and circuses. Reality show hair pulling and Jerry Springer chair throwing. It's all about the screaming. The histrionics. Saying the most vile thing you can think of because it'll get eyeballs on TV, views and likes on social media, or bump you up in the podcast rankings.

Snarling, angry self-styled alpha males and sexual molesters. Blowsy old drunks, desiccated also-ran prom queens, snarky, privileged trust fund brats, and nepo baby fascists. Rabid, snake oil salesmen. Jesus grifters. Dweeby, goofy, badly dressed incels on couches with the hot woman who'd never date them. Perky, hate-filled Barbies. Punks, skunks, and drunks. These are the people delivering "the news." Or maybe we should just call it "news wars."

RACIST MAGA.

In theory, America never should have needed a civil rights movement for the simple reason that the United States of America _is_ a civil rights movement. The extent to which anyone has had to fight for their civil rights is the extent to which the country isn't living to its promise.

Racism is in our blood. It's in our DNA. Part of our national psyche. The KKK. John Birch society. Lester Maddox. Strom Thurmond. David Duke. George Wallace standing in the doorway of the University of Alabama trying to prevent two African-American students from getting a college education, while proclaiming, "Segregation now, segregation tomorrow, segregation forever." It turns out Appomattox wasn't a surrender. It was just a temporary ceasefire.

MAGA is still pissed that the South lost the Civil War. Or "the war of Northern aggression," the remnants of which still lurk in statues, flags, symbols, and in the minds of their descendants. Part cultural. Part geographical. Part emotional and psychological. Yes, things have gotten less horrible, but to say we've made progress on racism is like saying a guy went to prison for raping five women, then when he got out he only raped three, so … progress.

Obama's election simultaneously drove them underground while dialing up the old-time hate. But instead of donning white robes and hoods they disguised themselves as neo-patriots with tri-coroner hats, holding signs about getting government hands off their Medicare. Turns out the hicks were right: The South did rise again. Bless their little hearts. And Trump was their boner pill, especially after Charlottesville and his "very fine people… on both sides."

But we've now entered a new era of American racism. Denial. It's gone beyond the original sin to the sin that never happened, and even if it did happen it wasn't so bad 'cause it was actually a vocational program for slaves who learned valuable, post-emancipation life skills. History is literally being whitewashed as school districts ban books and prohibit teaching it.

So, don't torment kids about shit they had nothing to do with 'cause it will only make them feel guilty, as teachers hover over them, screaming in their little faces, and ordering them to confess their White privilege, which is usually after they pick a gender, but before they're sent back into the arms of their parents in the pick-up line, assuming they haven't been shot during the school day.

It's fascinating that the White folks who declare themselves superior are the most inferior folks imaginable. Dumb. Poor. Angry. Violent. Uneducated losers clinging to their last vestige of their fragile identities: paleness. It's the only thing they've got left and they're not giving it up without a fight.

## GUN MAGA

All that is wrong with guns in America can be found in one brainwashed, doughy little bastard -- Kyle Rittenhouse -- a pathetic little teenager who'd been indoctrinated by MAGA media, whipped up with a false sense of urgency, seduced by the illusion of self-importance, armed by his mommy with an AR-15-style rifle, driven to the scene of a violent protest and told to defend the country by killing strangers, who then tried to grift off the moment by morphing into a media monster and right wing celebrity. We created this dangerous little shit, but had he been unable to get his baby fingers on an automatic weapon, he would have been reduced to using his words, which is usually what we tell children when they're having a meltdown.

We just love our guns. Love to own 'em, collect 'em, clean 'em, show 'em off, shoot 'em. Love them guns to death, and ain't no one gonna take 'em away. With over 400 million guns for around 330 million people, we are, per capita, the most heavily armed country in the world.

We're not just hunters in the woods blowing Bambi's head off or shooting birds out of the sky for fun and dinner. I'll give a pass to sport shooting and marksmanship, because the targets are actual targets. Not other people. (I have nothing against deer hunting, as such, but if the price of gun ownership is the daily American carnage then maybe hunters should just grab a knife and chase the deer through the forest. Might make it more sporting and they could also work in some much needed exercise.)

We have more gun fatalities per year than any other "civilized" nation, with over 48,000 deaths in 2022. That's around one death every 11 minutes. More than half were suicides. It doesn't say much for our way of life that we feel we need to go to such great lengths to protect ourselves from each other.

When we hit the fifty-ninth anniversary of the Kennedy assassination there were two mass shootings in the U.S. One at a gay nightclub in Colorado Springs, another at a Wal-Mart in Virginia. Interesting how some cities are going on their second or third round as locations of mass murder.

What is our problem? England lives without guns. France. Italy. Japan. Despite any romantic minuteman notions, they're not protecting regular citizens against a totalitarian government. If you've hit totalitarian, it's too late for citizen guns. See Russia. China. North Korea. A few scrappy *Red Dawn* kids scampering around the woods with automatic weapons aren't going to fight the actual power.

The typical pro-gun argument is that it's our 2nd Amendment right to own them. Former Supreme Court Chief Justice Warren Berger wrote that "The gun lobby's interpretation of the Second Amendment is one of the greatest pieces of fraud, I repeat the word fraud, on the American people by special interest groups that I have ever seen in my lifetime." And he was right. But we're so gullible that the weapons industrial complex still gets away with it. The U.S. gun industry rakes in around $9 billion annually.

There's also the weird intersection of Jesus MAGA and gun MAGA. The Colorado Springs nightclub shooter had a history of marital problems and threats against his family. Maybe a red flag law would've prevented him from getting his hands on an automatic weapon. After the shooting, his father, a former porn actor, was concerned that since it was in a gay nightclub, it could have indicated that his son, the shooter, was gay. He was relieved to find out that wasn't the case, as he's a self-proclaimed Mormon and conservative Republican.

No civilized society needs guns. Nobody needs guns. Most of the world manages to live together without guns. Except us. It may be our tradition but it's a suicidal tradition. It's a flaw in the system. We're not gun lovers. We're gun freaks, playing out some twisted power fantasy. We've taken it way beyond sport and hunting to full-metal mania.

And just to make sure that the horror continues 24/7, a Texas-based company is installing ammo vending machines in grocery stores, so that if you wake up at 3 a.m. with a desire for Oreos, and the urge to kill someone, you've got one-stop shopping. America will never be unfed, or unarmed.

## JESUS MAGA

A little over 2000 years ago, a Jewish mystic preached a message of love, compassion and tolerance and for his sins was arrested by the state and executed. And now the takeaway from that event has been lost in a multi-thousand year-old game of telephone, from the Inquisition, the Crusades, and Salem witch trials to the moral majority, and the modern era of Christo-fascism.

A commercial for Jesus aired during the 2024 Super Bowl, entitled "He Gets Us." According to Forbes, "the $20 million spot, (which also ran during the 2023 Super Bowl), was originally funded by the Servant Foundation, a non-profit fund that does business with The Signatry, a Kansas-based organization that networks donors and has collected $1 billion in contributions.

The claim was that the ad was part of an effort to improve the image of Jesus. Funny, I thought his image was already pretty solid. I didn't think he needed rebranding. One of the backers of the initiative was billionaire David Green, the founder of the craft store Hobby Lobby. The same Hobby Lobby that prevailed in a 2014 Supreme Court case in which the company contended it didn't have to pay for its employees to get contraceptives or "life-terminating" medications because it went against their religion. (Parenthetically, as Hobby Lobby is so hooked on Jesus, I'd think the last thing they'd want to promote is woodworking.) Still, it seems the only rule about Christ Club is that you never shut up about Christ Club.

Roughly 30% of Americans are Jesus freaks, including the Speaker of the House, who claims he and his son monitor each other's porn intake on a phone app. If God is omniscient, then what makes you think you can hide anything from Him? What makes you think He doesn't see everything you're doing, in whatever closet you're doing it? Let alone what's deep inside in your heart.

But MAGA Jesus is not historical Jesus. Not Sermon on

the Mount Jesus. He's more Book of Revelations Jesus. Angry Jesus. Vengeful Jesus. Gay-hating Jesus. Hell-fire and damnation Jesus. Armageddon Jesus. Rapture Jesus. White, English-speaking Jesus. The son of the God who created the universe yet is fine with polluting it. The son of the God who created sex yet hates it. That same omniscient sky daddy who had a kid via magic sex with a virginal married Earth lady then crucified the kid as a life lesson to everyone, but is sending the kid back to Israel where, according to The Book of Revelations, he will literally take up the faithful into the sky to a magical place, leaving everyone else to burn in fiery pit of hell for all eternity. MAGA Jesus loves Israel because it's Jesus' landing pad for the resurrection so they're terrified that Democrats will give away the store to the Palestinians because somehow if Jesus came back from the dead he wouldn't be able to get there because all the Muslims would turn it into a hot landing zone.

And then there's Mormon Jesus, based on the fable that the son of God got in his DeLorean and time-travelled to upstate New York in the late 19th century to leave secret-coded messages to a new Gospel on some buried tables that were discovered and translated by a local con artist. Oh, and he left a few rules behind, like no caffeine, alcohol, or pre-marital sex. But there's a green light on polygamy. Mormons even created the ultimate in sexual workarounds – soaking. Again, it's based on the arrogant, delusional notion that you can hide from an all-seeing God.

Jesus MAGA isn't an ideal; it's an identity. A private club. It's a symbol of White Christianity. You can point out all day long that Jesus wasn't White and it won't matter. Their Jesus is White. And he doesn't like sex, abortion, gays, or Jews. But he loves money and guns.

Jesus MAGA is rooted in the Moral Majority movement of the '80s, concocted by pompous ass, Jerry Falwell and the *700 Club's* Cryptkeeper lookalike, the late Pat Robertson. The '60s and '70s sexual revolution and Roe v. Wade decision caused a conservative right wing freak-out. Every movement for liberation is inevitably met with blowback by those who aren't prepared for the change in social mores or whose personal sense of identity is threatened. Evangelicals were all pissed off but had nowhere to go. The Reagan revolution was their political Viagra.

Fallwell and Robertson called 9/11 God's revenge for homosexuality and abortion. You'd think the creator of the universe, if he didn't like homosexuality or abortion, wouldn't have invented those things. And if he did but was having second thoughts he could've issued a position paper or written an Op Ed in *The Times* instead of, you know, murdering 3000 people and terrorizing an entire country.

Jesus MAGA also has a sex problem. These people base their lives around a literal reading of a dusty old book rooted in the ignorance and prejudices of a bunch of camel fuckers who lived in deserts halfway around the world thousands of years ago.

Jesus MAGA believes women deserve to be punished for sex. And pregnancy. That they are God's baby vessels. Rent-controlled apartments. These are people who think the Salem witch trials didn't go far enough. People who think legalizing gay marriage is somehow an imposition on their "faith," based on the notion that the creator of the universe, amid what must have been a chaotic time, what with creating trillions of galaxies and everything in them, could still micro-focus on the sanctity of heterosexual marriage. Even if the world is 6000 years old, as they comically contend, marriage is only around 4000 years old, which means that, according to their beliefs, there were roughly 2000 years of illegitimate fucking going on.

Jesus MAGA wants to fight the culture wars. They don't want abortions or gay or trans people but they do want guns and they don't care if you see that as a contradiction. And they're all made in God's image. In that case, God must be a fat fuck carrying an assault rifle into a Burger King, Church, synagogue, or elementary school. Or a scrawny kid stealing daddy's AR-15 and trying to shoot a presidential candidate.

Jesus MAGA believes there's a God who loves them but who spies on them 24/7. A God who created an entire universe but has time to listen to each and every one of their little prayers. A God who gets mad, sometimes acting out like a petulant child. These are people for whom Christianity isn't an ideal; it's a private club.

That's why Trump is their political Jesus. Their savior. The more they poked him with sticks, the more nails they slammed into him, the more they believed. It was faith, transferred to politics. Democrats don't see it. They throw up their hands in amazement. How can religious people support Donald Trump?! But they still live in a world where hypocrisy is a political mic drop. They don't see that for MAGA, Jesus, it's not about religion; it's about identity, empowerment, and fear of change. For them, the Bible isn't a book. It's a prop. A weapon.

In 2020, when Trump cleared the protesters out of Lafayette Park and held up a Bible in front of St. John's church, it was a shout-out to Jesus MAGA. He knew exactly whom he was talking to.

## SELF-LOATHING GAY(?) MAGA

Lyndsey Graham. Larry Craig. Mark Foley. Matt Schlapp. Josh Hawley. Ron DeSantis. Madison Cawthorn. Jim Jordan. Tim Scott. Mike Pence. Tony Perkins. Denny Hastert. Ralph Reed. Nick Fuentes. Roger Stone. Joel Osteen. Ali Alexander… are all men about whose sexuality I have no knowledge. Nor should I as it's literally none of my fucking business.

I have no idea if their wives are beards, and if their kids are props. I have no idea if their mystery girlfriends and sudden engagements after decades of "confirmed bachelorhood" are just performative face-savers to fool what they think is a gullible public. I have no idea if they grope male staffers or limo drivers at conservative events, participate in DC cocaine sex orgies, or solicit male attention in airport bathrooms, when they may, in fact, just have a wide stance. I don't know if they are secret cross-dressers. Many may just be stylish metrosexuals and not men with secrets buried deep in their hearts, or boys who look like they were born to wear rented powder blue tuxedos while chaperoning their cousins to the prom.

I'm definitely not saying that the evangelical Speaker of the House is so anti-gay his name might as well be My Johnson. I'm not saying that when Mike Pence speaks he virtually outs himself. He smiles, then drips out his points in this smooth, arrogant language, while simultaneously shaking his head "no" from side to side, as if his subconscious is screaming: "Don't believe a word I say! I'm living a lie!"

I'm not saying that their lives are a sham, that their kids are hood ornaments and that their wives made Faustian bargains in exchange for power and attention, to the point that in their annual Christmas photos they should be wearing actual beards. I'm not saying that the lives they project are a living desert of secrets and lies.

It may simply be a case of basic human biology and hormones slamming into repressive American culture. Men who were reared in the dogma of the evangelical or Catholic church, having it drilled into their heads at a young age that homosexuality was a sin in God's eyes.

However, much in the same way casinos calculate the odds on every spin of a roulette wheel, the human hormonal dice roll carries with it a similar predictability. While most of us are born with specific equipment that is in sync with our physical and hormonal make-up (aka cis gender) – and even though that hormonal makeup exists along a sliding scale within the boundaries of what we call masculinity and femininity -- in a certain percentage of people there's a more extreme variation. People born with one set of parts who are attracted to people with the other set of parts may be the majority of the population, but it's not all of the population. People are hard-wired differently. Given that, they have to find a way through life. Whether that's being open about their feelings, or denying them in public while pursuing them in private, or changing their designation by taking hormones and adding or removing parts, it's just people having a human reaction to what they feel inside.

But not everyone's able to do that. Barely a day goes by without some scout leader, youth minister, police officer, wrestling coach, conservative political leader, or local pastor getting outed for possessing a collection of kiddie porn, or getting caught with his pants down with an altar boy or sexting some teenager. While "pedo" has become an all-purpose attack word, it's most often thrown around by the very same MAGATs who are posing for ugly sweater Christmas card photos with their extended families. It must get pretty stuffy in that closet they all meet in, unless it's a secret speakeasy type entrance to a raver with lights, thumping techno and a disco ball.

It's a sign of their conflict and desperation that some people think they can pray the gay away, bleach it away or bully it away and still be accepted by people who hate them.

As the Westboro Baptist Church of Topeka, Kansas used to scribble on their signs: "God hates fags." I'm guessing that wasn't a direct quote either from God or lifted from either testament. Somehow the notion that if their God was so against gay people he had the choice not to create them, has escaped them. But gay people exist; therefore, by their logic they were created by the same God who made them. But we're not in a world of logic. We're in a world of fear and self-loathing.

On the surface, MAGA is a sexual prig. But double-secret MAGA is even hornier and more perverted than average people because their world denies them the chance to be who they are. Which is why they are at war with themselves but take it out on the rest of us. The more they hate, the more they date. The louder they scream; the louder they scream. There is so much rage there sometimes I wonder if the entire GOP isn't living on the down-low. It shouldn't be surprising that the busiest people at CPAC or the Republican National convention are gay male prostitutes.

Simply put: some people are gay, or somewhere on the LGBTQ spectrum. And it doesn't matter where they live, or what race or political party they belong to. It's also not affected by one's religious affiliation, no matter how a particular organization tries to beat or shame it out of them. Because some of these people end up in Republican politics, they tend to keep their inner drives hidden. They either hate women, are afraid of women, or secretly want to be women. People seem to think they can hide the gay away not just from other people, but from the God they claim is omniscient and created them. And that is some serious hubris.

On the surface, there's nothing about being gay that necessitates that one can't also be a fiscal conservative and a Republican, though it would seem that there's an element of compassion that might enter in the mix. Look at the Log Cabin Republicans. One can be physically and emotionally attracted to someone of the same gender and still can be for low taxes, less government regulation, and a cautious approach to foreign military engagement. But when the party is so blatantly against your rights to be who you are, it's tougher to thread that needle if you're in any way trying to lead an honest life. Of course, if you're only trying to get power, everything's off the table.

## ALPHA MAGA/ INCEL MAGA

These overly aggressive, self-proclaimed Alpha males grunt, groan, flex, and whine while waxing nostalgic for the good old days where men controlled everything. The more power women get, the more insecure and angry they feel.

To express their collective angst, they either band together in paramilitary groups, host podcasts, or rant on X/Twitter or Substacks. This is gnarly, grotesque, despicable, dumb, deranged, angry, ugly Alpha male MAGA. The ones who consider themselves *ubermenschen*. To disabuse them of that fantasy they should simply look in the mirror. They're predominantly White, self-proclaimed raging heterosexuals. Though their affection for tight T-shirts makes me wonder, given the preceding chapter, if some of them doth protest too much.

They seem to fall into two distinct groups: the seemingly steroidal, iron-pumping, self-described Alphas. Dan Bongino. Elmer Stuart Rhodes. Alex Jones. Enrique Terrio. Catturd. The Poor Boys and Goat Fuckers. The ex-military type alpha dudes who carried flags, fire hydrants, pitchforks, and bear spray, and howled like wounded bears at the Capitol.

And then there's the whiners. Those for whom Jared Kushner is their living Gumby god. Charlie Kirk, Kyle Rittenhouse, Ben Shapiro, Tucker Carlson. Ben Domenech. Dinesh D'Souza. Nick Fuentes. James O'Keefe. Steven Miller. Guys who look like they went in on a Groupon for extra gums and balloon heads.

Not that we're all born beautiful. Most of us do the best with what we've been given -- eat, exercise, dress well, make money, develop some sort of personality and sense of humor and figure out what traits are engaging to members of the desired gender. And while most people fall somewhere on the spectrum of moderately attractive to generally not Hunchback of Notre Dame hideous, others just wear their ugly with pride and make a virtue out of it. They also seem to be constantly pissed off at the notion that someone somewhere is getting laid and it's not them.

They also slide into racism and anti-Semitism, and are fond of dressing up in Best Buy sales associate outfits and white face coverings while carrying original 13-colony American flags and marching defiantly down the main drag in someone else's town, like they did in Charlottesville, then in Charleston, and more recently in Nashville. Oddly enough, they're often transported to these marches packed inside U-Haul trucks. As they seem to have the intelligence of furniture, I guess that's not surprising.

These legions of dorky agitprop artists seem to be in it for the cash, the fame, and the chaos. Political pyromaniacs who just want to watch it all burn down in the hope that they'll get famous and desirable by default. They sometimes band together, referring to themselves as the alt-right, but since they grunt, howl, and posture like Marvel Superheroes, maybe they should just rename themselves The Unfuckables.

## IVY LEAGUE MAGA

This is a perplexing phenomenon. One I've tried to figure out during long, morning walks and conversations with friends. Most MAGATs are dumb. Either ignorant, stupid, or both. But it's not just a movement of intellectual trailer trash. It's not just a dumb thing. It's a hate thing. Along with an arrogant, Caucasian thing that falls somewhere between cultural elitism and the divine right of kings. It's the people Tom Wolfe referred to in *Bonfire of the Vanities* as Masters of the Universe. It's the closest Americans come to being to the manor born. More like to the McMansion born, even though to old money Europe, even our old money is new money.

Exposure to an Ivy League education doesn't necessarily result in kindness, compassion, or social intelligence. I guess it's what results when Ivy League educations encounter minor league minds and souls, and over-privilege, often with the sidebar of a bad childhood. And the Republican party is their political domain.

Scampering Josh Hawley, Stanford and Yale Law. John Kennedy, who, despite the fortuitous name, has a Harvard education but does his best Louisiana cornpone shit when he's in public. The words drip down the side of his mush mouth like gravy sliding off a slab of cornbread. Just his arrogant way of playing to the base. Lindsey Graham, University of South Carolina law school. Tom Cotton, Harvard Law. Ted Cruz, Princeton undergrad, Harvard Law. Cruz was a master debater, which only proves that he is a cold-hearted cynic who arrogantly uses his rhetorical skills to confuse, not clarify.

Ron DeSantis. Yale. Harvard Law. Little Florida Napoleon in all his five-foot-five inch glory and cowboy boots with 3-inch lifts. With the Disney princess wife, they auditioned to be America's answer to Ferdinand and Isabella Marcos. Or Juan and Eva Peron. DeSantis looks like Augustus Gloop, the gluttonous chubby kid in Willie Wonka, with chocolate smeared all over his face. He tried to become neo-Trump and got almost gleeful bragging that if he got into office he was going to start slitting throats. Even as a metaphor it was over-the-line violent.

J.D. Vance, Yale Law. Wrote a book about the nobility of rural poor people then fucks them over in public. He once called Trump America's Hitler then turned around and blew him for an endorsement, on his way to garnering the VP slot.

Even Elmer Stuart Rhodes, founder of the Oath Keepers, now serving an 18-year sentence in federal prison for seditious conspiracy and evidence tampering related to the events of January 6th, was a graduate of Yale Law, though he looks for all purposes like your standard issue right wing thug, complete with an eye patch. Imagine your name is Elmer and you still think you have the standing to assume a leadership role in this country. Elmer is a brand of glue and the mascot is a cow. Vivek Ramaswamy, a rich Harvard grad who fancied himself enough of a rapper to try to spit Eminem, whom I pray meets him one day and stomps the shit out of him.

They all affect the posture of regular folks, but their backgrounds are far from it. There are two sides to this phenomenon: The arrogance of elitists who think they can trick voters into thinking they're one of them. And then there's the wish fulfillment expressed by poor, desperate outsiders who vote for the ultimate privileged insiders.

Interesting how these Ivy league grads fail to learn the lesson of history, which is that people who are struggling, tend to rise up and revolt when they have nothing to lose. And that often ends with cutting off the heads of those who were oppressing them.

Education is not only supposed to refine the mind but should soften the soul. Give one a broader outlook on the human condition. Maybe lead to compassion. It doesn't always work that way. Sometimes it just gives people with black hearts and empty, broken souls the skills to screw over everyone else. All *noblesse,* with none of the *oblige.*

GRIFTER MAGA.

The venn diagram of MAGA evil is, at times, a perfect circle. Many of those in other categories also fall into grifter MAGA. Opportunists who may share their beliefs but are just in it for the hell they can raise, the people they can fool, and the money they can steal. Villains, thieves, and scoundrels who know a good con when they see one, caught somewhere between greed, megalomania and misanthropy.

Roger Stone. A man with all the subtlety of a Batman villain. Most every Republican perversion rolled into one. Crook. Liar. Propagandist. A smug, arrogant freak with a Nixon tattoo on his back. Sometimes I wonder if Nixon drew it there himself.

Rudy Giuliani. Self-promoting former NY mayor, who ran around the country picking his teeth with the bones of 9/11 victims, trying to get elected president, then rolled over and went full MAGA, peddling insane election theories while the hair dye ran down his face and he Covid-farted on his co-counsel. Busted by Borat. Successfully sued for slander by the Georgia election workers he defamed. Rudy's now broke, and on his third divorce, from his cousin, no less, and is hawking his own brand of coffee. Upon his death he should be ground into dust and scattered outside the Four Seasons Grain and Feed.

Alex Jones. A snarling, rabid, hairless dog crossbred with a boiled ham, with a voice that sounds like he's gargling nails. A community college dropout, and TV snake oil salesman selling products called Brain Force Plus, DNA plus, and Knockout Sleep support. Someone who was found guilty of defaming Sandy Hook parents and was supposed to pay $1.5 billion but filed bankruptcy and is trying to weasel a much smaller settlement.

Then there's pock-marked Steve Bannon and his fever dreams of deconstructing the administrative state. Fancy Leninist language for anarchy and dictatorship. The winner of the Herman Goering look-alike contest. I'm sure every night as Bannon drifts off to sleep he fantasizes about invading Europe and stealing all the art and champagne he can lay his fat, stubby fingers on. It's easy to imagine Bannon at a Paris café drinking Dom Perignon while his boy band minions plunder the great art of Europe and ship if off to rot in the basement of his Bavarian villa.

There is something evil about the joy thugs get from secretly possessing great art. They know they can't create it, as their souls are destructive and not constructive. But there is a secret perverse pleasure in hoarding it, owning it, and denying the world the pleasure of experiencing it.

Bannon may not believe a tenth of what he spews out but he loves the attention. He loves the bombastic presentation. He gets a rush out of the momentary illusion of self-importance. Despite a seemingly ever-expanding beach ball gut, Bannon is rocking the bloated alcoholic bearded face, as he struts down the courtroom steps into the eager arms of cameras and jerks himself off in front of the media he so claims to despise.

He and Trump may have butted heads in their on-again off-again criminal rom-com, but it still comes down to game respects game. After snubbing his nose at a Congressional subpoena, it looks like he'll be out of jail before the election. He'll do his time proudly and emerge a conquering MAGA hero. His arrogance will get him through, while his whale fat will protect him from being shivved on the yard, and his pock-marked hideousness will keep him safe from predators.

And if there was ever a MAGA poster boy, someone who incorporates all of these characteristics in a single human being, we had George Santos. Or whatever his real name was. Grifter. Alleged con artist. Gay, not gay. Former drag queen. Check thief. Phony charity thief. Santos lied about his past and present, and still got elected by voters in his Long Island district. And after getting stripped of his congressional seat, he showed true MAGA balls and screamed about running again, before he gave that up. Next stop: The Masked Singer.

Dishonorable mention goes to Diamond and Silk. The female Amos and Andy of their generation. One of them is dead. Doesn't matter which. And the Blacks for Trump guy who seems to be at every rally, positioned behind the stage for maximum effect. Add to the mix Robert Kennedy, Cornel West and Jill Stein, whose third party candidacies could cannibalize the Democratic vote in November. I hope the Rubles they're getting are worth it.

## ZOMBIE BODY SNATCHER MAGA

In *Invasion of the Body Snatchers* aliens secretly invaded a small town and when the unsuspecting townsfolk went to sleep, pods were hidden in their basements and grow into an exact replica of the person, but with an alien agenda. A soulless replica of their former selves. This explanation is as good as any for the striking transformations that have taken place in formerly sane, or seemingly sane people.

Kari Lake – Former Phoenix newscaster and Obama supporter who lost her run for Arizona Governor then went full Trump, claiming it was rigged and continued to commit to the bit way past its expiration date. With a big smile and exuding all the slick confidence of a skilled card mechanic she can recite the "2020 election was rigged" canon by rote in order to rile up the base. Over a month after it was over she was still exhorting her followers to go to any means necessary, including violence, to stop Katie Hobbs – the incumbent who beat her – from being certified as the winner. From the soft focus camera shots to the insane Trump sycophancy she's even too nuts for Trump, She's now running for the Senate seat vacated by Democratic fly girl, Kyrsten Sinema.

Lara Logan – Former *60 Minutes* journalist who was sexually assaulted while covering the Arab spring uprising in Egypt. Don't know if it's PTSD or the Botox talking but she's gone full metal MAGA.

Ron Johnson. Russia Ron. Once a standard-issue conservative, now a salesman for Russian nesting dolls. He's so bleeding obvious with every public statement he should be wearing a ushanka, and holding a bottle of Stoli, while dancing the Kazatsky. Johnson is either a victim of brainwashing, blackmail, old-age crankiness, or senility. Or perhaps some lethal cocktail of all of them.

Rand Paul. Someone needs to get a power drill and back out the screws holding in Paul's toupee. They're clearly touching on his brain.

Ronnie Jackson. Once upon a time, he was President

Obama's physician. Then he was Trump's White House Dr. Feelgood. He's now the doppelganger for Jim Carrey's Fire Marshall Bill character. Seems there's an unrequited love thing happening for a former boss because this guy is just infatuated with Trump. During the days he was Trump's doctor you could almost see animated hearts fly out of his eyes when he told a gaggle of news reporters that Trump was the healthiest president in history and will probably live to be 800 years old. He's fanboying his former boss on Twitter and outside Trump's New York City courtroom, perhaps forgetting that he has a day job as a Texas congressman.

Megyn Kelly. Once penalized for asking Trump a harsh question about his comments about women, he retaliated with the old school slam about her being on her period. Post-Fox, she flirted with respectability by hosting a show on NBC, but was cancelled due to genuinely horrible ratings. She now hosts a radio talk show and podcast and has regressed to full MAGA. She looks like what happens when you put Botox in a 3D printer.

Matt Taibbi. Once *Rolling Stone's* neo Hunter Thompson, the scourge of Goldman Sacks, he did some time in Moscow and suddenly went full RFK using his verbal powers and skills to tout truly loony conspiracies.

Whether it's political opportunism, or Russian Kompromat, these people have morphed from seemingly competent professionals to raving, screaming MAGATs. Russia seems to know how to mix a special Kool-Aid that allows them to get their hooks into American journalists and politicians.

# LEFTOVER
# MAGA

Back in 2015, after Trump was done saying Mexicans are bringing drugs, and crime, and they're rapists, he softened the insult by saying, "and some I imagine are very fine people." So, I'll say the same.

Despite all the freaks, there seems to a group of Trump supporters who are working class people who just don't like paying taxes. Or maybe they don't agree with what's being done with their taxes. Ok, no one likes paying taxes, but most of us accept it in exchange for the roads, bridges, police, firefighters, and air traffic controllers. Or maybe they think the extremes of the culture war, the Me Too movement, and what they call "cancel culture" have gone too far. Every movement for liberation has that radical wing that gets oppressive in their insistence on ideological purity. Others may just be traditional Republicans and will vote party line no matter who the candidate may be.

Some are aging boomers. The Woodstock generation didn't last because the rebellion of youth will most often fade away when it slams into real life. It was always part reality and part illusion. The usual generational shift. In this case it was a passage from the war-torn '40s to the placid post-war '50s. The job of children is to rebel against their parents and proclaim their individuality. Hence – the counter-culture '60s.

The whole "man of the people" thing was just what was in the air. Poseurs on college campuses trying to fob themselves off as revolutionaries. Not all pot dealers were hip, young pot dealers. Some were just businessmen serving a new market and wearing a different costume. Much of it was the romanticism of youth. The ones who were "forever young" did their best to hold on to their ideals, and tried to create a better world. The ones who were always old eventually just got old.

I was recently scrolling through Facebook just because it's on my social media tour between Twitter, Instagram, and

TikTok. Usually it's the typical look-at-me living my best life kind of shit. Vacation pix. Kids. Food. Career humble-bragging. Celebrity selfies meant to imply that these people are besties, instead of proving that for one brief, shining moment they shared the same physical space.

Then I came upon a political post from someone I used to work with and respected. Someone I gave credit for being intelligent. The post was a litany of Trump's January 6th talking points, from "he told them to be peaceful" to "he offered Nancy Pelosi 10,000 National Guard troops and she turned him down." He accused Democrats on the J6 committee of lying about everything and that Trump was completely innocent. It pissed me off. Then it just made me sad. I wondered what turned him, and why he was spouting all this shit. Or maybe he was always this way. I noticed in the comments that someone else had engaged him, but quickly gave up, as it was clearly pointless. I blocked the person and moved on. But it left me with the queasy feeling that it's not just the usual suspects. MAGA is indeed a multi-headed monster. But except for the flag-waving truck and boat convoys, they were mostly all sound and fury, blasting away on social media. Then came the 2020 election.

Based on the Warren Zevon song: *Send Lawyers Guns and Money*, Trump had already exhausted lawyers and money, contesting the election results while spreading the fart of a lie that it had been, in his words, "stollen." Over 60 court cases lost. Sending his greaseball, leaky hair dye fart monkey Rudy Giuliani and his deranged cohorts to barnstorm the country making the same maniacal claims. It reached the height of absurdity when Rudy and his Sancho Panza co-counsel, Jenna Ellis, staged a photo op at the Four Seasons Total Landscaping. But while they were stomping all over the law, they were still operating within it. Until January 6th.

January 6th was a paradigm shift. The day America attacked itself. The MAGA Frankenstein monster crawled off the table and ran amok, breaking into and marauding through the Capitol under the illusion that they could throw a monkey wrench into the proceedings, invalidate the election, and send it back to the House of Representatives, where they had the advantage. John Eastman and Kenny the Cheese Bro's deranged battle plan.

Trump knew the anger was there. He roiled it up. He told them to "come to D.C. Will be wild." He seized on the hate and resentment of his supporters and pointed it at the Capitol because he didn't want to leave office and be vulnerable to prosecution. To borrow and bend a line from the Kris Kristofferson song: *Me and Bobby McGee*: Treason's just another word for nothing left to lose.

# CHAPTER THREE

# JANUARY 6

# THE
# PARADIGM
# SHIFT

There have been events in American history that have dramatically altered our lives, forever changing who are as a people, and as a nation. Moments that shattered the American sense of security and altered our psyche to the point that the dates themselves have become shorthand for emotional atomic blasts and rites of passage. December 7th. November 22. September 11th. No longer just dates but moments that changed us as a people.

In most cases, presidents have seized those moments and spoken in ways that ministered to a wounded nation, focused the national mood, acknowledged the horror, and laid out a path toward healing.

Lincoln's Gettysburg address: "… these dead shall not have died in vain – that this nation under God, shall have a new birth of freedom – and that government of the people, by the people, for the people shall not perish from the Earth." FDR, after Pearl Harbor: "A day that will live in infamy." Gerald Ford, after Watergate: "Our long national nightmare is over." Clinton after Oklahoma City: "We have come to rededicate ourselves to the belief that we can build a better, stronger society, where conflicts are resolved peacefully…" George Bush on 9/11. "The people who knocked down these buildings will hear from us all…" (Ok, it led to two neocon-orchestrated mission creep wars, in Iraq and Afghanistan, but in the moment, it was empowering.) Barack Obama, after Sandy Hook. Facing an unspeakable horror, he lit a path forward by spontaneously singing *Amazing Grace*. That single moment transcended speechmaking and ascended into art.

Despite our momentary differences, these cataclysmic events have brought us together. Up to now, they were things that happened to us, whether the disasters were natural or man-made.

Then there was January 6th. This was different. This time, the attack was committed by the very person in the White House whose job it was to preserve, protect, and defend the Constitution. It was his job to protect us. Instead, he attacked us. The President of the United States launched an assault on our government in an attempt to invalidate a legitimate election, remain in power, and virtually overthrow the government.

In a previous book entitled *Death to America*, published in 2020, I stopped writing six months before the election and wondered how far Trump would go for power. I knew he was a deranged megalomaniac, but I still failed to take the advice of Robert Loggia's character in *Scarface*: "Never underestimate the other guy's greed." Though, in this case, it was his fundamental amorality, and criminality. Trump has always operated outside the lines. He'd push, bend, or molest the system as far as he could for his own benefit, but I never thought he'd try to blow it up.

His game has always been, "heads I win, tails it's rigged." Trump had been seeding the "rigged election" idea in the American mind since 2012, during his first run for office. This is what he does. He gets a catchphrase then rams it into the public consciousness. Brainwash, rinse, and repeat. "Can't release my taxes because I'm under audit." "Mueller was a witch hunt." "No obstruction. No collusion." "The Zellensky call was perfect." "The 2020 election was stolen." "It's a rigged system." "The ballots are rigged." "The New York hush money case was rigged. Mail-in voting is rigged." Why was he against mail-in voting? Because he was told Democrats are mail-in voters. Republicans are same-day voters. If it was the opposite, he'd be virulently pro mail-in.

He did it again in 2016. "I will accept the results of the election, if I win." He was continuing to set the table for the eventual outcome. He even encouraged his "people" to check polling stations in Philadelphia, planting the idea that there was something illegal going on with the voting process.

In 2016, he didn't need the con. He became president, then immediately set up the Voter Fraud Commission, headed by Kris Kobach and Mike Pence. It was disbanded after finding no fraud. The only fraud was the commission itself, the point of which was to further implant the idea in our heads that presidential elections can be rigged.

He even got his sclerotic old pit viper Commerce Secretary Wilbur Ross to screw with the census in order to disenfranchise urban voters for the upcoming 2020 presidential election, while trying to make a case for Voter ID, as he knew it has the same effect: voter suppression. He also sabotaged the USPS via Louis DeJoy who was last seen playing the villainous Mr. Potter in *It's a Wonderful Life* and who, for some uncanny reason, is still in his job. During the debates, he told the Proud Boys to "stand back and stand by."

He even invented a new chant, in the tradition of Build the Wall! Drain the Swamp! And Lock Her Up! Trump came up with "Stop the Steal." The allegation that he'd won the 2020 election was, and still is, a giant, Goebbels-style lie. But he pounded it into the national psyche. Pushed it to legitimacy via the power of repetition. Then he started coloring outside the lines.

He tried to get Secretaries of State to nullify the results in their respective states, including the infamous "perfect" phone call to Georgia Secretary of State Brad Raffensperger, asking for 11,780 mythical votes. Raffensperger had the foresight to record the call and release the audio. Trump has been indicted but will probably never go to trial.

Then there were the phony audits. Giuliani, and his traveling Medicine Show. The John Eastman memo was a blueprint for treason. Though *Atlantic* writer Bart Gelman wrote about this months before in an article speculating on the possibility of election results being overturned by sending it back to Congress and the individual states. (It was not the first time a candidate thought about trying to throw an election to the House of Representatives. Strom Thurmond tried it in 1948. George Wallace again in 1968. But they were third party challengers, hoping to stop the major party candidates from reaching 270 electoral votes.)

As a quick sidebar: I've yet to hear anyone answer this question: If the Vice President's role in certifying the vote count is purely ceremonial then why would an election be nullified and sent to the House if he was unable or unwilling to perform that function on that day. What if he was in the hospital or unavailable for some other reason? Is the system that flimsy and fragile that the election gets tossed? If the officiant at a wedding gets in a car accident on the way to the ceremony does that mean the couple can't get married? What if Pence had gotten Covid and was in the ICU? Would that have nullified the results? What if he went along with the scheme? I'm sure there's a valid answer to this question. I just haven't heard it.

In America you're allowed to lie. You're allowed to propagandize. You're allowed to claim an election was stolen. You're allowed to challenge election results in court and lose over 60 times. You're allowed to hold a rally and scream your fool head off that you were robbed, as your supporters raise their flags and pitchforks in defiance against what they've been told is injustice.

You're not allowed to entice or extort election officials to fake the vote count. You're not allowed to whip up slates of fake electors and collude with congressional allies to overturn the results. You're not allowed to attack the government in an attempt to prevent an election from being certified. You're not allowed to attack police officers. You're not allowed to threaten the life of a Vice President and members of Congress. That's treason. It's also attempted murder but let's put that one aside for the moment.

Behind the scenes, Trump was bending the rules, trying to force himself on the system. His version of deflating the football. After all his efforts to contest the election failed, Trump still could have left office in the classic way. Gracefully concede. Promise to help your successor in every way to do the work of the American people. Smile for the Oval Office photo op. Attend the inauguration. Do the big wave from the stairs of the plane then fly off into the sunset. Do speaking tours. Write the obligatory book. Plan a library.

(Although Trump's library will be more of a book burn-pit. The last thing in the world he wants are his presidential papers on display. He's either stolen them, eaten them, sold them, or flushed them down the toilet.)

But he didn't pull an Al Gore. He didn't concede, pack his shit, and go home. Instead, he attacked. On January 6th he was a quarterback who was chased out of the pocket then ran out of bounds, took off down the sidelines, knocked over cameramen and cheerleaders, then leaped across the goal line and declared he scored a touchdown. It didn't matter that it was all on video and refs were throwing flags everywhere.

Trump summoned the rake and pitchfork crowd to D.C. They were dumb and/or angry enough to go. They didn't' really know what they were doing other then grunting and growling about wanting their country back. They wanted to hang Mike Pence. Kill the "Demoncrats." One attacker suggested on the floor of the House: "Let's sit down and pass some shit!"

If it wasn't so tragic it would have been comical. The cast of the movie *Freaks* trying to overturn an election. Treasonous congressional Republicans, right wing extremists, paramilitary maniacs, toothless, rando trailer trash, 'roided-out high school dropouts, fat, angry, malcontents, shady lawyers and, to cap it off, the wife of a sitting Supreme Court justice all conspiring to pussy grab power.

For all the investigations, hearings, subpoenas, testimony, indictments and impending trials, we still haven't gotten the words right. Donald Trump didn't "foment" a riot, "incite" an insurrection," or stage a "coup." He launched an attack. He summoned his supporters to D.C for the "rally." He tried to pressure state officials and threatened his Vice President. And when he wouldn't go along with the scheme, he tried to have him assassinated. (Pence is being celebrated for doing the right thing. In truth, it was the one time in his years as VP that he didn't do the wrong thing.)

These weren't two distinct phenomena. The president. And then the crowd that he whipped up. They were one thing. One plot. And it was planned ahead of time.

In December, 2020, he fired Defense Secretary Esper and hired Chris Miller as acting Secretary. Miller issued a memo on January 4th neutering the D.C. National Guard's ability to respond. On January 5th, the leader of the Proud Boys was at the White House. There was a self-described "war room" at the Willard Hotel with 25-30 plotters, including Bannon, Giuliani, Michael Flynn, Roger Stone, Bernard Kerik, Boris Epshteyn, and Christina Bobb.

Trump fired up the crowd to fight. To march to the Capitol, but they were essentially the background extras. He already had his shock troops moving in. This was the plan. The fuckers even showed up in matching riot gear. It was not a spontaneous attack. Many of them had gas masks, bear spray, and zip ties. And they had a cache of weapons nearby. No one takes bear spray to a peaceful demonstration. If that had been BLM the bodies would have littered the Capitol steps.

And Trump wanted to be there. He's a Hitler fetishist. In his mind, that was his Reichstag burning, along with his march into Paris under the Arc de Triomphe. He attacked his limo driver and fought off the Secret Service detail. He disputes the claim, but with Trump it's usually fair to assume that he's lying and that the craziest shit you've heard is true.

Trump attacked his own government. The difference here was that, unlike the many women he attacked, this time the system didn't back down. You could call him the mastermind, but he wasn't smart enough to conceive it, or clever enough to plan it, but he was crooked enough to execute it.

He had his braintrust. The deranged, mush-mouthed Sydney Powell, crazy Lin Wood, deranged pillow salesman and former coke fiend, Mike Lindell, slimy Rudy, Covid fart victim Jenna Ellis, Stevie "Three Shirts" Bannon, Steven "Renfield" Miller, our American Goebbels, Alex Jones, Mark Meadows, mini-psycho Michael Flynn, ambi-sexual Zippy the Pinhead look-alike, and Batman villain Roger Stone. This collection of miscreants should be stalking the halls at Comic Con, not determining the course of the nation.

Then as they invaded, some members of Congress

colluded with the plot, and others protected themselves, called for help and waited it out, while Trump watched the proceedings on TV for 187 minutes with his crooked family. Even his kid's girlfriend preened and did her grotesque Velociraptor dance for the camera. Many have accused him of doing nothing, but that's not accurate. He was doing something. He was waiting to see if the plan would work. No matter how many people got hurt, or killed.

Only when Pence called for backup and the riot was quelled did he record his feeble surrender message. "We love you. You're very special. Now go home." Even with his forced speech he radiated contempt for his people. He talked to them the way people talk to the special needs kid who just tied his own shoes.

And when the crowds left, the House reconvened and certified the election. Only then did he take his shit, the ho-bag wife, the slimy kids, along with 15 boxes of top secret documents, and split for Mar-a-Lago to lick his wounds, grift for money and plot his return to power. And here we are.

Donald Trump committed treason. He did it in plain sight. Call it insurrection if that's the legal term. But he didn't "incite an insurrection." He launched an attack.

Only after it failed did the cadres of young blond believers on the White House staff realize there may be something unhinged and amoral about the boss. But most of his Republican operatives played along with the lie and when it didn't work they tried to minimize it or re-brand it.

This was not "legitimate political protest" as Romney spawn and former RNC head Ronna McDaniel tried to spin it. It wasn't an FBI false flag operation. He didn't offer 10,000 troops to either Nancy Pelosi or Nikki Haley. It wasn't peaceful. It wasn't a spontaneous riot. Ted Cruz used his snarky debate skills to declare that there were "Thousands of peaceful protestors on the lawn that day." That's typical Cruz bullshit. Truth: There were thousands of people at the rally. 2000 broke into the building.

Five people died as a result of the attack. Four members

of the U.S. Capitol Police ended up committing suicide. 174 officers were injured. 1300 people have been charged with crimes. 749 have received sentences. 467 are in prison. Trump recorded God Bless America with them, calls them "hostages," and is promising to pardon them all. Once upon a time, as Trump himself has brought up, traitors were shot. Or hanged.

Waiting for Merrick Garland to act was interminable. Like waiting for Godot. Or, in this case -- Godarland. By comparison it felt like Godot would eventually show up. It was echoes of Bobby Three Sticks and the first impeachment.

In the aftermath, Trump did what he's always done. He worked off the Roy Cohn playbook. Use the system to game the system. Deny, deny, deny. Never confess. Never admit anything. Fight. Stall. File motions. Delay. Threaten to sue, accuse your enemies of doing exactly what you're doing. Threaten judges and their families. Flood the zone with lies and counter-narratives and confuse the media, let alone the jury pool. Spit in the eye of the legal system. Propagandize. Confound the public with inflammatory social media posts and erratic rallies. Bribe or threaten judges. Or put them in your pocket. Spit in the eye of the truth, and live to lie another day.

He lies to his people because they will believe it. They want to believe it. Americans have never been used to being lied to in this way. And on this level. We're not Russians. We haven't built up decades of cynicism and distrust. Our bullshit detectors are not as finely tuned.

Trump still remains unscathed for January 6th. Thanks to his allies on the Supreme Court he will probably never go to trial. He installed his plastic daughter-in-law to head the RNC and is grifting like a madman.

Ideally, the January 6th trial should have been Trump's last stand. It should have been the game changer. Again, that's not on him. That's on us. We are the Disunited States of America, and we're locked in a battle between the rule of law and a dictator wannabe who knows returning to power is his only way to stay out of prison. The question remains if the system will withstand the assault.

As we head for the 2024 election he's ahead in many polls, particularly after the debate, and the shooting in Pennsylvania. Although the game completely changed when Joe Biden pulled out and anointed Kamala Harris. Trump's conviction in the New York hush money case may have lead to him momentarily losing some support. But it didn't stick. He'd successfully delayed the other trials and the Supreme Court took care of the rest by granting him virtual retroactive immunity. Still, after all he's done should it really take a trial to convince people of his criminality? What hasn't he done? Hasn't he been rapey enough? Traitorous enough? Criminal enough? Clownish enough? Lethal enough?

He's now trying to delay any January 6th evidentiary hearings past the election at which point, if he loses, he'll keep fighting or take a midnight flight to Moscow, assuming he's of any use to Putin after another loss. If he wins, the cases will all disappear. Forget any legal distinctions between federal and state charges, or any judgments that have already gone against him.

The treasonous bastard isn't even cos-playing democracy anymore. He's not dictator-curious. He wants absolute power. He wants to be a dictator on day one, and take revenge on his enemies. If he manages to lie, cheat, and steal his way into the White House there's no doubt he'll take the oath of office wearing Qaddafi Ray-Bans, and a soldier suit, festooned with ribbons and medals, which were awarded for his bravery and sacrifice fighting his own personal Vietnam in the AIDS-tainted '80s New York club scene. And there'll be a Jumbotron image projected behind him, straight out of North Korea, along with the obligatory goose-stepping, phallic missile parade.

If he gets back in power, it'll simply be: "Come and get me." Scarface meets Fuckface.

# CHAPTER FOUR

# WHAT THE RIGHT GETS WRONG

There's an old joke about politicians stranded in a lifeboat in the middle of the ocean. The seas are heavy, the boat is taking on water, and the sharks are circling. The Republicans wrestle with the decision of who to throw overboard to lighten the load and divert the sharks, while Democrats spring into action and appoint a committee to study the problem.

Democrats think. Republicans act. Democrats fall in love. Republicans fall in line. Democrats trust reason, argument, Socratic method, and the idea that the truth is all that matters, and most importantly, that it will set you free. Republicans believe we're already free and don't need to think about stuff they've been told to believe in. Like low corporate taxes. And the Bible.

Democrats think words matter. Thoughts matter. Ideas matter. Facts matter. Policy matters. And they do. When you're in power. But when you're trying to get power or keep it, they don't. I wrote this in 2016 and it still holds true: The worst thing you can call a Democrat is inconsistent in their position, or, horror of horrors, a hypocrite. The worst thing you can call a Republican is out of power. And. they will do or say anything to get it and keep it.

The American thrill is gone. We agree on nothing. The Right thinks the left are all athiests who only care about DEI, CRT, BLM, and LGBTQ, checking their White privilege, transgendering their bathrooms, killing their faith, raising their taxes, exporting their jobs, opening their borders, taking their guns, aborting their fetuses, and grooming their kids.

The Left thinks the Right are all women-hating, gay hating Jesus freaks who think social programs are about creeping socialism.

It's worse than non-communication in a bad marriage. It's not just that we don't get each other's jokes. We don't like the same music. The same movies. We don't talk with each other. We talk at each other. And we don't listen when the other one talks. We don't spend quality time together. We're coming at life from two different realities. We speak two different languages. We don't understand each other because we interpret the other through the prism of our own worldview.

We used to agree on the country's goals: life, liberty, and the pursuit of happiness. We agreed on the destination, although we disagreed on the directions. It's no longer a matter of how to get there. We don't even agree on where we're going.

We're two countries, two cultures, living in separate states and in two different realities. It's Athens vs. Sparta. Platonists vs, Sophists. Id vs. Superego. Where Truth isn't Truth. And lies spew out of a platform called Truth Social. They're even inventing their own flags.

As noted, MAGA comes in all shapes, sizes, and income brackets, with smaller subsets clustered in specific geographic areas and of specific gender varieties and skin pigmentations. There are Blacks for Trump. I even imagine there are a few of them who aren't being paid. There's Hispanics for Trump. Probably some cultural misogyny and old-school Jesus going on, though why they would vote for this *pendejo* remains a mystery to me.

But putting aside the various permutations, let's just be frank: most of them are poor to lower middle class, non-college educated White guys. And the following is directed at them.

What the fuck is wrong with you people?! Republicans have been trying to kill you for years and you still vote for them. They take your health care and you vote for them. They send you to fight misbegotten wars and you vote for them. They refuse to take care of you when you come home wounded and you vote for them. You get sick from cleaning up burn pits and they won't take care of you. And you vote for them. They didn't care if you risked your life cleaning up the toxic waste dump that was the World Trade Center and got cancer and needed medical help. Republicans stonewalled against that legislation until Jon Stewart shamed them into voting for it. And you still vote for them.

They lie to you every election cycle and you vote for them. They whip up your fears, and play on your insecurities, and you vote for them. They screw with your markets and you lose family farms, and you vote for them. They're coming after your health care, Social Security and Medicare and you still vote for them. They don't just want to privatize it. They want to eliminate it. They want to eliminate you. And you still vote for them.

You're fed this lie that Republicans are better for the economy, yet three times in the last 100 years, Republicans and their policies have crashed the American economy and sent us spiraling into recession or depression. There was Hoover, during the Great Depression. FDR rescued the country via the New Deal. Bush, during the housing market crash of 2008, and Trump in 2020 when he tried to bullshit his way past a disease. And two of those last three times, Joe Biden was integral to the country's recovery and return to prosperity. And you wear T-shirts with the logo: "Let's Go, Brandon." Seriously, what the fuck is wrong with you?

Donald Trump is not an aberration of the Republican party. He's the endgame of the Republican party. He tried to kill you at least six times while he was in office and you want to give him the job again.

1) Trump tried to make you sicker and poorer by getting rid of the Affordable Care Act all because Barack Obama insulted him at the 2011 White House Correspondents' Dinner. He came within one Republican vote of doing it. Millions of people would have suffered all because of his tiny, bruised ego. And it took a Republican to stop him. John McCain, in the final stages of cancer, was most likely sending Trump a pre-emptive fuck you by dramatically voting it down at the 11th hour. That's how close Trump and Republicans came to making your lives hell. Even then Trump lied, saying he'd unveil a "fantastic" health care plan in two weeks. That was seven years ago. And he wants to kill it again, using the same line of bullshit. And he may get away with it because you motherfuckers keep voting for him!

This is health care. Health care is not a Republican thing, or a Democratic thing. It's a human thing. Everybody gets sick. Everybody will need medical care. And based on the system we have everyone except the super rich will go broke from medical costs. It's the American solution to the human condition. Either you get killed with astronomic medical bills or enormous co-pays and go broke, or you get killed with cancer. And, based on actual life, this will happen to everyone. And that's just following the natural progression of things, which is that people tend to get sick when they get old, which is also when they stop working. But what happens if someone in their forties loses their job and gets sick? Or their kid gets sick? Tough shit.

As long as Republicans have demonized government run health care as "socialized medicine" and invoke "government death panels, (fuck you, Sarah Palin), we're dooming ourselves to death or poverty. Or both.

2) Trump also tried to kill you by stealing the Supreme Court and getting rid of Roe v. Wade. He did this. He bragged about doing this. Millions of American women are going to suffer and he is responsible. And now he's trying to weasel out of it.

3) Trump stole from you by giving tax cuts to the top one percent, playing the same trickle down economics game, popularized by many other Republicans who also tanked the U.S. economy. His economy was not the "greatest economy in the history of the world!"

His economy rode the wave of the Obama/Biden recovery, then he juiced the stock market with tax cuts for the richest 1%. His people even tried to sell them using the stale "trickle down" bullshit, which even the creator of trickle down economics has debunked. Doesn't matter. Like an old Halloween costume, Republicans store "trickle down" up in the attic and dust if off when the season comes around. The stock market went up almost 300% under Obama/Biden, and only about 30% under Trump.

He also destroyed the lives of farmers by hitting China

with tariffs so they couldn't sell their crops. Many ended up losing family farms and even killing themselves. He's threatening to do this again. And he may get the chance, because you motherfuckers keep voting for him.

4) Trump tried to take your freedom by colluding with a foreign dictator and sworn enemy of the U.S., both to influence the 2016 election and by selling out NATO, which would make us weaker overseas and, eventually, weaker at home.

5) Trump tried to kill you by lying about Covid. He knew it was deadly yet he said it was contained. He said it would stop at 15 cases. That it would disappear like magic in the Spring. It's now over 111 million cases. He said everyone would get better. There have been over 1.2 million American deaths, and many could have been prevented if he hadn't convinced people to let their guard down and not wear masks or get shots. Like Herman Cain.

Herman Cain, Godfather Pizza CEO and presidential aspirant was too caught up in the world of political power to think straight. He had a failed presidential run in 2012 and probably thought he could ride a unique origin story, and corporate success back into politics. So, he attended a Trump super-spreader rally in Tulsa before it was medically advisable, and didn't wear a mask. He was diagnosed with Covid two weeks later, and died.

Trump killed him. Like he almost killed Chris Christie by neglecting to tell him he'd tested positive during their 2020 debate prep. He wound up in the hospital. And fuck you Chris Christie for thinking Trump deserved your help in preparing for the debate. And also fuck you for stumping for him in 2016, even grandstanding at the convention. You make the noises of an ethical, intelligent man while doing the most unethical things. Then you return in 2023 thinking you could carve out an anti-Trump lane to the nomination.

Trump literally killed Americans by slow-walking Covid and railing against taking protective measures. This time he didn't only poison the American mind, but murdered actual Americans. Including Republicans.

6) Trump tried to take your freedom by attacking American democracy while trying to overturn an election. He got Ashli Babbitt killed. He's responsible for all the deaths, injuries, arrests, and convictions that happened as a result of January 6th. He conned his people into breaking the law so that he could stay in power and out of prison.

And now you're ready to re-elect him?! What the fuck is the matter with you?! Trump told you he loved the poorly educated. He called you stupid and you voted for him. Which makes him right. At a Vegas rally in 2024 he told the crowd not to pass out from the 104-degree heat because he needed their votes, but didn't really care if they died after. He even told a crowd in 2016 after the election that he didn't care about them because he no longer needed their votes.

Your party doesn't care if you die. They don't give a shit if you die. They don't give a shit if you work forever with no benefits and no sick leave, no workers' comp and no unemployment insurance and have a heart attack and die. They don't care if you die in a mine explosion or in a plane crash. They don't care if you lose your job and your health insurance with it and then you get a disease and go broke trying to survive. They don't care if your wife has an ectopic pregnancy and bleeds to death in a hospital parking lot because your deranged Doctor Strangelove dead from the waist down and the neck up Texas Governor hates women. They don't care if your kid gets cancer. As far as the party is concerned you're just a replaceable part in a machine.

As the newly elected Jesus freak Speaker of the House, the self-loathing ventriloquist dummy and generically American-named Mike Johnson proclaimed: "Women need to have babies to add more workers into the work force." To them, women are citizens until they get pregnant, then they're incubators. Baby factories in the human/worker supply chain.

As former Republican political consultant and full time never-Trumper Stuart Stevens wrote as both the title and premise of his book: "It was all a lie." To paraphrase H.L.

Mencken: "No one's ever lost power underestimating the intelligence of the American people."

# CHAPTER FIVE

# WHAT THE LEFT DOESN'T GET RIGHT

Republicans constantly get played by their own party. Candidates travel to their states, put on a pair of mom jeans, cowboy boots, an open-collared shirt and a cowboy hat, then stand on a bale of hay and fake being a man or woman of the people. Then they finish the speech with "God bless you and God bless the U.S.A. Then they stand around for a few selfies, get back in the limo, roll their eyes, and race back to the hotel suite for a cleansing shower to remove the stink of honest people, then climb into their silk pajamas, order up a steak and a bottle of Cabernet from room service, jerk off to a picture of Ronald Reagan, then turn out the lights and try to erase the dread of having to do it all over again the next day.

Democrats, on the other hand, are all too fucking noble, telling their humble origin stories as if they were the lyrics to a political love song to romance blue-collar voters into thinking they're just regular folks. If they ever spent a summer on their grandpa's farm or had a part-time job in a factory in high school, or were raised by a single mom who worked three jobs, you can bet your ass you're going to hear about it in the first five minutes of a stump speech. It's their working man bona fides. The opening aria in the Democratic opera. It's usually the prelude to them rolling up their shirtsleeves and walking around a local diner, asking people's opinions, and nodding as they pretend to listen.

Then, once they feel accepted by the plain folks, they launch into a recitation of past and present policy positions and 10-point PowerPoint plans to perk up the economy. They also love alliteration because they think it amuses people and captures their attention.

Joe Biden came into office, distributed the Covid vaccine, put money in everyone's pocket, did an infrastructure bill, and put the tanked economy back on its feet. The stock market is higher than it's ever been, no one's talking about recession, inflation is coming under control, and unemployment is at all-time lows. And still Americans are under the perception that Republicans are better on the economy. That's because Democrats suck at politics. They don't know how to fight. And they don't know how to sell. They couldn't sell oxygen on the moon. They keep thinking that the American people will wake up and see how much Joe Biden's done for them. They won't. They have to be told.

There's an old adage in advertising: "Nobody reads body copy." It's just about the headline. The message. The theme. The gestalt. But Democrats never seem to get it. Democrats campaign in body copy. Policy. Bullet points. Charts. Graphs. White boards. Statistics. They assume everyone will have to vote for them once they comprehend their positions on the issues.

Elections are not about policy. They're about politics. Down and dirty politics. Politics is power, power is policy, and policy is life. (See Roe V. Wade. See the Supreme Court Immunity Decision.) If you don't win politics, you don't get to do policy. Policy may be noble and fact-based, but politics is ignoble, volatile, and chaotic.

When Democrats win it's because life hands them the perfect candidate at the perfect time, like with FDR, JFK, Jimmy Carter, Bill Clinton, and Barack Obama. Along with an imperfect opponent.

Democrats win elections in spite of themselves. For all our posturing, and self-congratulatory chest thumping when Biden won in 2020, patting ourselves on the back for restoring goodness and decency to American government, righting the ship, ending our national nightmare, and eliminating the stool that was Donald Trump from the alimentary canal of the body politic, we were wrong. And we need to get one thing straight as we steamroll toward the Super Bowl of political clusterfucks that will arrive on November 5th, 2024: Trump could have won in 2020. Easily. He basically screwed himself.

## TRUMP COULD HAVE WON

Trump is the dumbest human being I've ever seen in public or private life. His stupidity is almost comical. And he's not even clowning in private, or for the sycophants who hang out at his Palm Beach roach hotel. He's clowning on the world stage.

But Trump is also an idiot savant. And the savant part involves his unique ability to act in his own self-interest. He has a rat-like instinct for doing whatever will fend off danger and ensure his survival. Except in 2020 when he fucked up and made the wrong play.

Let's do some drunk history. Go back to late 2019/early 2020, when we began to hear the rumblings of a virus coming out of China. Covid 19. Not, as Trump spokes-hack and Leni Riefenstahl-wannabe Kellyanne Conway claimed, that it was the 19th Covid. It was the year 2019. And cases in Europe were rising rapidly.

On the front page of the *L.A. Times*, dated January 27, 2020, beneath the tragic headline of Kobe Bryant's death, was an article about the first two cases hitting California, along with cases cited in Arizona, Washington, and Chicago. Of course, since our thinking is so linear, and since the virus originated in China, Trump put a limit on travel from China, ignoring the fact that all it would take to transmit the virus would be one tourist flying from Beijing to Rome, who coughed on someone going to London, who then sneezed on a traveler going to New York. It was inevitable that it would hit the U.S. because germs don't recognize national borders.

In a February, 2020 phone call, Trump told journalist Bob Woodward that Covid was "Bad. More deadly than your… more strenuous flus." "You just breathe the air and that's how it's passed." He added: "It's not just old people," and "this is deadly stuff." He knew all this. He just neglected to tell the American people. Trump said he played it down in public because he didn't want to cause a panic. That was bullshit. If you're crossing the street and an out-of-control car is racing toward you, panic is the appropriate response. Followed by getting out of the way.

Trump's people must told him that the economy would virtually shut down as we hunkered in place trying to avoid getting sick. He played it down because it was an election year and his plan was to run on the economy. "The greatest economy in the history of the world!" Which it wasn't. He's still selling that same lie.

Put aside doing the right thing. A normal president would have handled the crisis responsibly, by focusing on the health and well-being of the American public. He would have made the case that we are all in this together. That mask-wearing protects us all. That health care professionals with decades of experience are giving us sound advice and we are all doing our best to learn as we go.

He would have urged people to take care of themselves, their families, friends, neighbors, and coworkers. He would have brought us together, talking about toughing out hard times and the indomitable American spirit. This would have been patriotic bullshit 101.

But Trump went with his natural instinct: Lie and deny. He tried to hoax it away. He called it the "China" virus. He said it would go away like magic in the Spring. He mocked mask-wearing. He demonized his own health care experts. In February, 2020, he accused Democrats of politicizing the virus, calling it the new "Democrat hoax." He mocked reporters for wearing masks.

He battled his own experts. He said it was over. No danger. He said, "It's only 15 cases and pretty soon it will be down to none, so that's a pretty good job we're doing." He got Conway and Larry Kudlow to declare it was "contained." He claimed he was good at this medicine thing because he had an uncle who went to MIT.

We soon found ourselves faced with the horror stories of overrun ERs, shortages of ventilators and tests, along with the sight of refrigerated morgue trucks. In our post-vaccination world it's easy to forget the horrors of early

Covid.

But he stayed with his perceived self-interest and his instinct to fight reality by continuing to bullshit germs. But the germs weren't having it. He even tried to crowbar open the economy around Easter because he figured in his tiny lizard brain that the Christian contingent would appreciate the resurrection metaphor. The problem was, it wasn't going away. Cases were on the rise everywhere. Then he actually got Covid. Then he gave it to Chris Christie and almost killed him. He even tried to give it to Joe Biden in the debate.

He tried to get people to go back to work. To church. To school. He suggested, on live TV, that we inject bleach into our bodies and point our assholes at the sun to allow the healing rays of light to get in.

This is how his tiny, childish mind works. Since we knew at the time that the virus could be killed on surfaces with bleach, or outside via direct exposure to the sun, he made the mental leap that the same theory would work inside the body. He might as well have reasoned that since putting gas in a car enables it go 80mph that if a person drank gasoline, they'd be able to run 80mph. This is the mind we elected to the presidency, and are considered re-electing.

He pushed Ivermectin, a horse de-wormer, and Hydroxychloroquine, even claiming he took the latter. People followed his advice and died. You know he had a financial stake in the company or some scam worked out. He never hawks something that hard when there isn't money in it. Even in 2024 he's still selling it.

Meanwhile, as they spun their little fantasy, reality refused to cooperate. Cases rose. Deaths rose. Businesses closed. We had food shortages. People scrambled for groceries and toilet paper. Masks were so scarce we were urged to save them for health care workers. ERs were overrun. Doctors and nurses were exhausted, that is when they weren't getting the disease themselves. The sound of ambulances became the music of the night in many cities. It was a total shitshow. Something we hadn't experienced. But Trump held firm with denial, lies, and bullshit. He attacked the NIH, CDC, and demonized China to the point that Asian people were being attacked on the street in this country, because that's how dumb we are. He said mask wearing was voluntary. In late May the death toll neared 100,000 but he still wouldn't mask up in public. In June he wanted to stop testing so we'd have fewer cases, another example of a child's mind at work.

We were locked in our homes. Unemployment shot up. We were scared. Leaderless. Only when cases were rising and the public was frantic did he begin to relent. Then in May, 2020, he gave in and established the Coronavirus task force. Operation Warp Speed. But it was way too late. It had already spread throughout the country and shut everything down. That's where his lies took us.

Now… Imagine, if you will, that he had taken the virus seriously. Imagine if, in early 2020, he did an Oval Office address to the American people: "My fellow Americans. This virus is bad. It can kill you. Protect yourselves. Protect your families. Mask up. Be careful. We'll get through this together, etc…"

Since his supporters simply followed orders they would have listened to every word he said. They would have become the mask police, stationing local lunatics outside every store, school, bowling alley, mall, supermarket, and strip club demanding people put on their masks. And they'd make sure they were at least KN95s and not cloth. And no gaiters or bandanas. It's not fucking Woodstock. They would've stormed Walmarts for every mask they could get their hands on.

If Trump had lauded the work of Dr. Fauci, the same idiots who threatened and continue to threaten his life would have been building statues to him. That's how dumb these people are.

Then, imagine if he also said, "The experts say it will take 12-18 months to get a vaccine. I, however, with Operation Warp Speed" will deliver a vaccine this year." It wouldn't have mattered at the time whether it was true or not. He would have come off protective, and defiant, an iconoclast who refused to accept what the experts told him. He's going to work his Trump magic and make it happen sooner.

Then came the news of the MRNA vaccine. Even though it didn't arrive until December 2020, we knew help was on the way. And he could have taken credit for it. And the same anti-vaxxers who shrieked about putting a foreign substance into their bodies would've been the Vax Nazis, storming CVS, bulldozing their way to the front of the line and demanding shots for themselves and their families. They also would have stationed themselves in public like the Gazpacho police, demanding to see vaccination cards: "May I see your papers, please."

He could have come off like a leader guiding the country through rough times. Sure, he opened up the Treasury threw some Trump bucks at us, just like he tossed foul shots of paper towels at Puerto Rican hurricane victims. It wasn't his money. It's was OPM. And if there's one thing this asshole knows it's OPM. He doesn't care if blew a giant hole in the deficit. It was necessary to get us through the crisis.

Trump could have fobbed himself off as the hero who guided the country through Covid, like FDR guided us through WWII. Then, with money in their pockets, a vaccine on the way, and the argument that Trump protected and saved everyone from the virus, they would have voted for him en masse, and he would have been re-elected. Probably in the very same landslide he claims he got.

He would never have had to go through the lawsuits, crazy Rudy's hair dye and Covid farts. No January 6th. Just four more years of Trump, and we'd be looking in 2024 at the Ivanka/Jared ticket. Or the end of the 22nd Amendment. Or the end of free and fair elections. Or Putin-style elections where he wins with 110% of the vote, and his opponents are murdered. It's ironic that, this one time, Trump failed to calibrate his self-interest and realize that the truth would have set him free.

So, before we go thinking how noble we were in

electing Joe Biden, a good man, and all the good work he's done since, remember that it was only Trump's bad decision that got us here. And here we are. After all the shit he's done, this election is still way too close. And after all the shit he's done, it shouldn't be.

Note: The previous segments were written over the past three years. But after the infamous debate fiasco of 2024, and the subsequent failed clean-up, and then the Pennsylvania shooting, Biden dropping out and passing the torch to Kamala Harris, the game has changed. And it's changing moment to moment. The following reflects both events that have taken place over the last several years, as well as our present reality.

## THE OCTOBER SURPRISES
## CAME EARLY

A presidential election is not a debating society where you win by making the better argument. It's not about clarifying your policy positions, or pointing out all the great things you've done for the American people. It's a street fight, mixed with a rugby scrum, with all the predictability of a pachinko machine.

In a street fight you win by beating your opponent. And Donald Trump is a creature of the street. But Democrats continue to campaign on the moral high ground, which may be the battle site of our 2024 defeat, and will go down in history with other moments when we failed to imagine the unthinkable, like Pearl Harbor, the Tet Offensive, 9/11, January 6th, and now June 27th.

As Donald Rumsfeld noted, at certain times in history, there are the known knowns, the known unknowns, and the unknown unknowns. Even in recent history, there have been October surprises. The Comey letter, which kneecapped Hillary's campaign and for which there was no effective counter. And there was the Access Hollywood tape, which seemed like a knockout punch but was deflected and beaten back.

The June 27th debate was a gut punch. It completely reset this election.. This was followed by the Supreme Court's decision in the immunity case, which put more wind at Trump's back. And then by his near savior-like status after surviving a shooting. This was soon followed by President Biden's withdrawal from the race and endorsement of Vice President Harris.

We knew the debate would be a proving ground for President Biden. We anticipated that there might be shaky moments. But no one thought he would crumble the way he did. The one moment that was designed to put to rest any doubts about his age and cognitive ability backfired. It made the opposite case. Even with Trump's 90-minute firehose of horseshit, the story that emerged was Biden's collapse. Democrats, as is their nature, went into full panic mode.

In early July, the decision of whether Joe Biden could be the Democratic party nominee hung in the air, as the media examined, discussed, and sometimes exacerbated the situation. Meanwhile, people on X/Twitter were going for each other's throats over whether we needed to stay the course or find a new candidate.

At that point, several things seemed certain: It didn't matter if Biden's performance was a singular event or an indication of a more serious condition. The optics were horrible, and the polls seem to reflect it. Even if Democrats took the Access Hollywood denial tactic, the only person who could have effectively launched that defense was incapable of launching it. This was a dangerous Catch-22. None of the clean-up was working and every day brought new supporters calling for him to pull out. Which he insisted he wouldn't do. And then he did.

As for the Supreme Court, one could say that the fix was in when they took the immunity case, and then stalled until their last day in session to issue a decision, but no one seemed to anticipate the severity of that decision and what it portends for the future of our democracy, particularly in light of the Heritage Foundation's dystopian 2025 Project.

The speculation now is who Harris will choose as a running mate. But no matter who ends up on the ticket, Democrats need to step up their game, and fight. So, here are ten modest proposals for Democrats. I'm not saying they're hard and fast rules. I'm just saying that if they don't follow them, we're going to lose and lose hard and our democracy will be dead and our lives will be over.

ONE: GET OFF THE MORAL HIGH GROUND. CAMPAIGN THROUGH STRENGTH.

Except in those rare cases, like with Barack Obama, honesty, sincerity, compassion, and intelligence don't win elections. Even then, it took a tanking economy, a hapless, slightly confused opponent, and his tactical error of picking an imbecile for a running mate, based on the premise of her being physically attractive and the fact that she was momentarily able to capture media attention and the national imagination until she outed herself with her own stupidity, leaving her vulnerable to being mocked on a late-night comedy show.

Democrats fell in love with Obama and they want that feeling back. Before the debate there was always someone on X/Twitter posting one of those get more follower questions like "how cute are puppies," or "how much do you love ice cream." The political version was: "If Biden doesn't run in 2024, who do you want?" The answers terrified me. Oh, the heartfelt, earnest wishcasting!

Elizabeth Warren! She's brilliant! Pete Buttigieg. He's smart, and gay married with kids! Bernie! Medicare for all! Gavin Newsome! He's handsome! Gretchen Whitmer! She's tough.

Democrats get a hopium high fantasizing about their ideal candidates. They think all we need to wake up the electorate is a light sprinkling of magic liberal dust. Hopefully, the debate and Supreme Court decision have blasted those people out of their utopian fantasy, and made them realize the necessity of dealing with our dystopian reality.

We need a new mission statement. Instead of all the hand-wringing and *geshreying* (Yiddish for yelling while worrying), over the horrors of Trump returning to office, Democrats need to rally behind the declaration that Donald Trump will never enter the halls of power again. Not vertically, walking into the White House. Not horizontally, lying in a box in the Capitol Rotunda. It's not happening. Never. He will be stopped. He will be crushed. He will be defeated. And the political ground where he lives will be salted so that no Trump, either by name or temperament, ever grows there again.

It doesn't matter who the nominee is, or what the polls are saying. Democrats need to not just show strength, they need to be strong. They need to stop moaning that Republicans don't care about acting in the interests of the

American people. That's not a damning indictment. It's the premise. They care about wielding power and staying in office. That's it. It's like we elected Al Capone mayor of Chicago and Democrats are throwing their hands in the air, wailing, "Oh, my God. It's like he has no interest in governing!" No. He doesn't. He's a crook. And we elected him. The job is to keep him from being re-elected.

Toward that end, there are two agendas: sell the Democratic nominee, and destroy Donald Trump. While everyone was focused on Biden's debate performance, and CNN's lack of real-time fact-checking, no one deconstructed Trump's side of the debate, the torrent of lies, and the danger he represents.

Trump needs to be destroyed in the public mind. Link him to great dictators in history. Bust him for Covid deaths and our 2020 economic collapse. Brand him as a convicted criminal. A rapist. Infuriate women with his sexual assault convictions and for killing Roe v. Wade. He's attacking women's health care. He's committing political rape. Link him to the Heritage Foundation's Project 2025. There's no such thing as going over the top. You have to scare the shit out of people. And you don't even have to make it up. Fear is a great motivator. Especially when the fears are based in reality.

You can't shame Donald Trump out of existence. In the real world Hitler doesn't have a third act revelation, where he sees the error of his ways and makes amends. In the real world the allies invade Europe and bomb the shit out of the Nazis. Then Hitler offs himself in his bunker to avoid capture. Trump needs to be ruthlessly beaten into submission. Politically.

TWO: STOP WHINING. STOP WISHCASTING.

Democrats still think Republicans are just bad Democrats. They think ideological consistency and hypocrisy matter. They don't. Democrats think their feelings matter. They're always outraged, aghast, infuriated, mortified, flabbergasted, appalled, clacking their tongues and shaking their damn heads like it's a fucking mic drop. They're always pointing out the irony of this or the hypocrisy of that. MAGA doesn't give a fuck. Democrats' reaction to Republican behavior is exasperation. "This is horrible. Immoral. Illegal! Won't somebody write a song parody or perform an interpretive dance?!" For a bunch of woke leftists and committed resisters they always seem to be one step away from an antebellum fainting couch. No one's ever been owned by a defiantly carried sign or rushed to the hospital with a third degree Twitter burn. Or, in a post-Elon world, I guess an overexposure to X-Rays.

And stop whining. "Why didn't the media given Joe Biden credit for all his accomplishments?!" Because it's not their job to give him credit. It was always his job to take it. You have to beat people over the head with what you've done in a way that they will understand. Fuck humility. If you brag about it, it must be important. Conversely, if you don't brag about it, it must not be. Especially in this race. It's about showing strength. Reason may be reasonable, but it comes off as weakness.

Democrats need to learn how to act like Republicans. That's how they stole the Supreme Court. McConnell denied Garland a hearing. He had nothing to lose with this play. Worst case scenario, Hillary won and appointed him anyway. Not what happened. Trump appointed Gorsuch. Then Trump blackmailed Anthony Kennedy into retiring. That gave us Kavanaugh. They even rigged the hearings by messing with the FBI investigation. Then RBG died, even though she should have retired during Obama's term. Another example of Democrats screwing themselves. Then came ACB. The result: the death of Roe v. Wade. And the immunity case decision. Republicans legally stole the Supreme Court and got their white whale. And with every legal win, Clarence Thomas plucks out a pubic hair, glues it to a Coke can, and uses it on his desk as a paperweight.

THREE. DEFINE THE BATTLEFIELD. DON'T GET BRANDED. BRAND YOUR ENEMY. ATTACK.

From Day One, this administration committed political

malpractice. From Day One, there should have been one consistent message coming out of the White House: "Trump and Republicans wrecked the economy. President Biden and Democrats are fixing it." Just like they did twice in this century. Once after the housing market collapse in 2008, and again after Trump tried to bullshit Covid. Each time, Biden was at the center of the rescue effort.

I'm repeating this because it should be repeated. Constantly. Every single event, plan, bill, law, shovel-ready project should have been a subset of that single message, so that even a downturn in the market or a rise in gas prices were subheadings of the greater narrative.

They should have set and managed expectations. We were coming out of a Trump-induced Covid lockdown and economic crash. We were locked up because the imbecile tried to bullshit his way around a virus. It didn't work. And we all suffered. But we're changing things. We're getting back to work. We're getting vaccines in people's arms and money in their pockets.

Once expectations had been realistically set, every event would have been explained in that context. Of course, at some point, the administration in power has to own the economy. But they keep citing statistics, forgetting the headline. Trump fucked it up. Biden is fixing it. You have to give the people a story. Then tell it over and over. Another adage from advertising, when pitching a campaign: "Tell them what they're about to see. Show them. Then tell them what they saw."

Republicans always work from the Karl Rove playbook: attack your enemy's strength, not their weakness. Democrats don't get the game. They don't know how to fight their way out of the branding box. This was even more poignant as we dealt with the debate fallout.

There was a time when the "Biden is old" meme might have been handled. The mistake was accepting the premise and then trying to disprove it by endlessly discussing it rationally. Biden's only four years older! Biden rides a bike!

If Republicans had claimed that Martian space lasers shot the voting machines and changed the 2020 results, Democrats would have gone about disproving it by bringing in Dr. Neil deGrasse Tyson to testify that he checked the night sky through the world's most powerful satellite telescopes and can prove that there was no evidence of Martian activity in our atmosphere anywhere around the time of the election. They totally miss the point. The attack is not about fact. It's about the insult. It's about weakening your opponent. It's a schoolyard taunt. A rap battle.

Yes, in truth, sometimes Biden carried himself as "old" so if there's an element of truth to the insult, it sticks. Just ask Low Energy Jeb, L'il Marco, or Lyin' Ted.

They could have said that Joe Biden is not "old." Calling someone "old" is an insult. It's not a statement of fact that describes something in objective reality. Like saying something is cold or hot. There is no definitive stage of life called "old." It's meant to imply that someone is out of touch, irrelevant, weak, confused, and powerless.

They could have said that Joe Biden is older…. than he was yesterday. As are we all. We get older every second. What he is, is wise, and experienced. A dedicated public servant. A skilled negotiator both in foreign and domestic policy. He's savvy. A steady hand. He's surrounded by a great team. He understands the needs of regular Americans. Sure, if you need to put out the video of Biden riding a bike, add that if Trump tried to sit on a bicycle it would disappear up his colon.

Democrats didn't make that case. They didn't communicate the idea that Biden was the general commanding the troops. He's not fighting in the trenches. The campaign slogan could have been, "Biden Works. While Trump cheats at golf." "Biden Works. While Trump sells gold sneakers." "Biden works. While Trump is in court being found guilty on 34 felony counts." Of course, this was all before the debate and his eventual withdrawal, but it's a lesson in political warfare. Don't allow yourself to be branded.

Of course, reality didn't help. Biden has never been a

skilled orator. He's always been clearly anxious about a childhood stutter so he tended to race through speeches, hitting the important points, but with no resonance. No music. Just a high-pitched string of words and sentences in which he often omitted the definite articles. He also carried himself with an old-man gait, crooked his finger grandpa-style, and sprinkled in phrases like "I'm not kidding around." Or "this is no joke." Even his old man shuffle on his way to the debate podium was instantly damaging.

His speeches needed to be shorter. Fewer words. Fewer tangents. More succinct. Simpler, broader themes. They needed to surround him with young people at every event, the way Trump paints the background of his speeches with the Blacks for Trump guy. It's not just the message. It's the messenger. And the optics.

Biden has always been much more effective one on one. There should have been more town halls and interviews, and fewer speeches. His debate prep was totally mismanaged. Too many facts. Not broader themes designed to brand Trump, who actually is old. And angry. Cranky. Mean. Doddering. Confused. Hysterical. Insane. Dangerous. He's grandpa at Thanksgiving after his third Scotch. He's your perverted uncle who brings the hug in too close, and lingers too long. He's dumb. He's deranged. He's dangerous. He's deadly. Just ask Herman Cain.

The political wisdom of agreeing to that debate and those terms -- that will be debated for years. But there is a lesson in it. Don't let your enemy define you or the terms of battle. And calibrate how your actions will play out in the country. If you're attacked, attack back. Don't accept the playing field as defined by your enemy.

FOUR. GET THE WORDS RIGHT.

Stop calling January 6th "the insurrection" as if it's damning in and of itself. The word is too fancy. It has too many syllables. And stop calling it a "Coup." It's a French word. *Coup d'Etat.* Americans don't like French things. French things make them feel stupid and uncultured. To most

Americans, "Coup" is the sound a pigeon makes.

Calling Trump an "insurrectionist" is soft. It's vague. It's as effective as people on the right calling their opponents globalists. It has no meaning; other than as a code word for "Jews." And once they think society will let them go back to using it, they will. As in "Jews will not replace us."

Stop referring to opponents as "election deniers." Stop trying to coin a phrase like "The Big Lie." They're all attempts at Trump-style branding by repetition but they're soft and they don't play.

Stop referring to Trump as an "aspiring autocrat." An "authoritarian." A dictator. This doesn't mean shit to the people you're trying to communicate with because they don't understand these words. Plus they sound powerful, which they like. They want power. They like being called fascists. Fascists are tough. Fascists carry guns. They arrest and shoot people. To them, it's a compliment, not an insult. Almost more importantly it plays right into the MAGA resentment against coastal elites. In the effort to make the case, it's self-defeating.

FIVE. TRUMP'S BASE SUPPORT IS NOT RATIONAL. IT'S EMOTIONAL.

Republicans are at war with a changing culture. They're freaking out over who goes in what bathroom or plays which sport. The latest in their grab bag of rants and hysteria (interesting word, etymologically) is their freak-out over Drag Queen Story Hour. I would defy anyone to demonstrate a qualitative difference between Drag Queen Story Hour and a Sunday sermon at the Vatican. And even though I know we could just have regular old story hour if we wanted, if people want to do Drag Queen Story Hour, or Lesbian Story Hour, or NASCAR Story Hour, then do it. Unfortunately, this phenomenon has been labeled by the Right as if it were KKK Story Hour, an event those of us on the Left would object to. So, we are at an impasse. The attack is working. So, if you know your enemy is going to attack you with Drag Queen Story Hour, maybe take a short reprieve from fighting for Drag Queen Story Hour and win the larger war so that we can get back to a world in which parents aren't losing their minds over Drag Queen Story Hour.

I recently heard a well-known prosecutor on a podcast join the host in bemoaning the pathetic state of our politics and the fact that Trump supporters are brainwashed, and that they support a guy who doesn't give a fuck about them. The guest remarked, "But how can you reach them?" What argument can you make to change their minds? There is no argument. And you can't change their minds. The mistake is thinking that this is about making the right argument.

MAGA is not based on an idea. It's based in emotions. Anger. Fear. Resentment. We laugh at the Trump pictures. Trump as Jesus. Trump as Rambo. Trump as Superman. Trump as Top Gun. They're all hysterical. Comical. Buffoonish. But the Trump imagery isn't realism; it's religious iconography. People are already getting tattoos of the post-shooting photograph.

In all these depictions Trump has six-pack abs, a thick mane of blond hair, and he's almost god-like. In this alternate reality, he's what he claimed to be when he was booked in the Fulton County election interference case. He said he was 6 foot 3 and 215 pounds. In reality, his left ass cheek weighs more than 215. But it doesn't matter. Not for his people. Not in their reality. He is their savior. And they won't give up fat, orange Jesus any more than they'll give up original Jesus.

Obama was right. They do cling to their guns and their bibles. He was wrong to say it out loud as it gave his opponents ammunition and confirmed their beliefs that the elites looked down on them. They're right. We do. But not because of who they are but because of how they act. And vote. Still, never give your enemy a bat to beat you with.

The QAnon invasion has reduced Republicans to the "The moon is made of green cheese" party. You can't combat this delusion by trying to disprove it with moon rocks and statements by scientists. You can't bring in astronauts who have landed on the moon, NASA engineers, physicists, and geologists presenting data about the actual physical composition of moon rocks. Republicans have been sold the idea that the moon is made of green cheese, their sense of identity is tied in a Gordian knot with the moon being made of green cheese and you'll have to pry the moon being made of green cheese out of their cold, dead hands.

SIX. LEARN TO FIGHT

Democrats have to learn how to use the power they have, when they have it. Democrats think if you speak loudly, and clearly to a MAGAT and lay out the logical case, they will be compelled by the force of your argument to come around to your side. No. They won't. You have to show strength. Not demonstrate moral superiority.

Democrats legislate to make life better for people. Republicans wield power to get what they want for themselves. In 2016, Mitch McConnell said he wouldn't give Merrick Garland a hearing to fill the open Supreme Court seat, because it was an election year and the people should decide. That was eight months before the election. In 2020, eight days before the election, it was "Amy Coney Barrett come on down!" And Democrats went insane. Contradiction! Hypocrisy! He lied!! We got him! No. You didn't have shit. Not in Republican reality. Mitch used the power he had and each time he said what he had to say to use it. Just like when he made the case against the second impeachment by stating that we still have the courts. We see how that turned out.

In the 2022 midterms, Herschel Walker was the Republican Senate candidate in Georgia. The man was an imbecile. A two-by-four. A block of wood. Not even functionally illiterate. Walker was as dumb as a rock. They might as well have run an actual rock. Walker was "hold my beer" dumb, though it's probably more charitable to take pity on him as he's probably suffering from some kind of CTE from his football career. He's the person for whom the Southern expression "bless his heart" was invented. It's no crime to be dumb. It's a crime to be dumb and run for the United States Senate. Of course, Republicans didn't care about him. They wanted to trade off his popularity in the state so that they would have his vote in the Senate.

Yet, in their attack ads, Democrats graciously tagged Walker as "unqualified" to be a United States Senator. How dainty and refined. Yes, it was the South, but c'mon. They should have buried him. Even though at one point on election night Walker was technically ahead, the remaining votes were from heavily Democratic counties so he wasn't actually winning. But, it should have been a blowout. He should have been laughed off the stage. What should shake every Democrat down to their shoes was that the race had even gotten that far, and that Republicans were cynical enough to run him.

Glen Youngkin, who won the Governor's race in Virginia in 2022, was the perfect phantom MAGA candidate. The carefully constructed "independent-minded" Republican in his maroon Mr. Rogers vest. See? It's sort of red, so you get that he backs Trump. But it's a vest, like Mr. Rogers, so he must be a nice guy and not an asshole like Trump who he fully supports but would never say so. Democrats should've tagged him immediately as a fake but they blew it, because they didn't know how to brand him and take away the power of his costume.

Youngkin campaigned on CRT – Critical Race Theory – and the idea that it was being taught to children in school. It was a fake issue designed to fire up voters. It was also a lie. CRT was a graduate level college course. But Democrats didn't call him out on it. And then, to complete the unforced error, Democratic candidate, Terry McAuliffe, a former governor, and an experienced, savvy politician, shot himself in the foot by declaring that parents should have no say in their children's education. He couldn't have said a dumber thing at a worse time. It played right into the CRT fable. That was a self-inflicted political gunshot.

Democrats' weakness is that they don't know how to fight propaganda. You can't fight it with facts. If modern American liberal Democrats were in Berlin during *kristallnacht* they would've hit the streets with signs proclaiming: "The

Jews are actually wonderful people!"

Democrats make passionate well-reasoned arguments on podcasts, X/Twitter, and TikTok. They think these arguments deliver a coup de gras. They use expressions like "coup de gras." They think calling Trump a fascist is a damning accusation when, to his people, it's a compliment. It means he's powerful. And they love that. His power is their power.

An early 2024 cover of *The New Yorker* showed a banana republic cartoon Trump complete with the Qaddafi soldier outfit goose stepping and throwing up the Nazi salute, and Democrats cheered like a blow had been struck. Like it was a real weapon. It wasn't. Roughly 1.2 million people subscribe to *The New Yorker*. I imagine most of them are Democrats. And even if a glance at the cover gave them a rush of validation, and the illusion of a powerful comment, I don't think MAGATs saw it as a slam-dunk argument. When it's a fight to the death, gentility and civility are not weapons.

And all this bullshit about "wokeism" is just that. Bullshit. It's a rallying cry for the right to employ the culture war attack by conflating the extremes on the left with the entire movement and the entire party. It's branding.

The left doesn't get that the right is easily conned. Just whip up the base with a slogan. Invent a problem. Benghazi! Hillary's emails! Caravans at the border! Antifa! BLM! CRT! Defund the Police! The deficit! Inflation! Transgender bathrooms! Grooming children! The Radical Woke Left! Hunter Biden's laptop! Hunter Biden's gun! Hunter Biden's dick! It doesn't matter. They just want shit to scream about. If one con runs out of gas, switch to another.

Trump's tactics must be used against him. Rebrand him. Show how he's tried to destroy the lives of his own people. He's a convicted felon! Put up ads showing how many of Trump's people have gone to prison like it's a chart of mob bosses. Go after moderates. Fire up women over Roe v. Wade. Go agitprop on his ass. Attack him at his rallies. Put up signs. Fly over him with banners. Stalk him at court appearances.

Throw him off his game. Show that he's vulnerable. Run the nastiest, ugliest, most old-school fear-mongering ads you can think of.

Hang him with getting rid of women's right to health care. Trump delivered the kill shot to Roe v Wade. McConnell blocked Garland, Trump gave us Gorsuch, Kavanagh, and Handmaid Lady. This was their holy grail. And after 49 years, they delivered. That is playing the long game. That is success. Trump takes credit for killing abortion when he's in Republican circles but is trying to tell the lie that everyone wanted it moved to the states. He's trying to tack to the left because he knows he's in danger of losing moderates and suburban women in the general election. Don't let him.

The life lesson here is not Edward R. Murrow's takedown of Joe McCarthy, Woodward and Bernstein's intrepid Watergate reporting, or the subsequent congressional hearings. We're way past "have you no shame" or "What did the president know and when did he know it?"

Also, from Inauguration Day, they also should have had Trump and his co-conspirators under 24-hour surveillance. I don't care how "police state" it looked. Trump's been railing against the deep state. So what if this one time the deep state actually snuck cameras and microphones into Mar-A-Lago and eavesdropped on every word he said. Let him scream and play Chicken Little. Who would care if this one time he was right. The Biden administration should have known everything he was up to and used it against him. I only hope they did and we just don't know about it.

I disagree with the Sun Tzu quote that if your enemy is destroying himself don't get in the way. No. If your enemy is destroying himself, put your boot on his neck and finish him off.

SEVEN. LEARN HOW TO SELL. RESPECT THE POWER OF SYMBOLS. RESPECT THE POWER OF THE MOMENT.

Build Back Better was a horrible slogan. Bidenomics was equally horrible. Alliteration and word play are not replacements for a real sales concept translated into an effective message. Dems think it is. If you mention the Chips Act, explain that it means jobs. Bringing manufacturing home. Americans don't know what the Chips Act is. They think you're talking about cookies.

Even the January 6th congressional hearings were all body copy. Compelling witnesses, testimony, and bombshell revelations. But no headline, which should have been: "Donald Trump is guilty of treason." Everything should have flowed from that one premise. Instead they treated the events of Jan. 6 and Trump's involvement and reaction as two distinct phenomena, instead of a single attempt to overturn a legitimate election and overthrow the government of the United States so that he could stay in power.

Democrats make fancy, clever signs at their rallies. Double, even triple entendres. Not to mention the t-shirts and hats they make their kids wear. Sometimes they match! Then they go on Facebook or Instagram and brag about the pictures of them holding their clever little signs. The only valid symbolic takeaway from Democratic rallies and marches were the visuals of the massive crowds themselves. They could see the crowds from space. But no one could read the fancy words on the signs.

And Democrats keep handing them victories like the president of Harvard who couldn't admit on TV that threatening to kill Jews at Harvard didn't fall under free speech. All she had to say was "it was hate speech and we condemn it" and then clarify her answer by making the larger point about the complexities of free speech at a university. But once again, academics are too fucking clever for their own good, thinking that analytic distinctions mean anything outside of academia. Stop trying to educate and learn to communicate. Especially in these times.

Trump knows presentation. In 2016, right before the first debate with Hillary, he staged his bullshit walk-back from the birther attack, at his DC hotel. He opened the show with Medal of Honor winners.

In another pre-debate sideshow he dragged out Bill's accusers and staged a press conference. It was also a shout-out to Bill and Hillary that he knew the rest of Bill's sins and wasn't above busting him. Trump absorbed the Access Hollywood tape and rebranded it as "locker room talk." The fact that he mentioned that he'd heard worse on the golf course with Bill Clinton was not just an idle remark. Again, he was sending a message.

Similarly, Democrats have to put on a show. Hardly a news day goes by without some Trump administration veteran doing an interview, usually to hawk a book, testifying how dangerous Trump is. They were in the room where it happened. These are interesting and important segments but as one-offs they lack power. Democrats need to put on a town hall or similar segment with every single Scaramucci they can get. BOMBSHELL! TOGETHER! TONIGHT! IN PRIME TIME! ON ONE STAGE! TRUMP VETERANS WARN THE AMERICAN PEOPLE! All those people together on one stage, selling the idea of how dangerous he is. The power is in the picture and the event.

With Kamala Harris running Democrats are re-energized. They need to take the fight to Republicans. Brand Trump as old. Turn it around on him. Put him on defense. Democrats need to create a simple narrative, represented by symbols just as clear and simple as MAGA. Democrats have too many clever ideas and fail to refine them into powerful symbols. The pussy hats looked dumb and were too ironic. You had to think about the meaning. Symbols, like jokes, have to work immediately.

The peace sign was a powerful symbol of the Vietnam anti-war movement. The raised clenched fist was a powerful symbol for the Black Panthers. "Yes, we can" was powerful because they captured the spirit of the times and the dynamic personality of the man. Slogans evoke emotions when they express a single, clear idea.

EIGHT. STOP PLAYING THE "THEY'RE NOT REAL CHRISTIANS" CARD.

Democrats think they've said something when they pull out a quote from the Sermon on the Mount or the Beatitudes and note the intent of the original passages when contrasted with the behavior of those who refer to themselves as Christians. They think they're scored a point. It's the same gotcha moment when they dig up an old Ronald Reagan quote and note how far modern Republicans have strayed from any noble original intent. These arguments don't matter. Republicans aren't living in a world of argument. They're living in a world of identity where Jesus means what they want it to mean – basically, God's on our side so our side's right. The Jesus they love is not the Jesus from the Beatitudes. It's angry Jesus from Revelations.

Don't think you've scored a point by noting their religious hypocrisy over abortion and guns. They don't care. They want guns, and they don't want abortion. You can point out that the 2nd Amendment was ratified in 1781, when there were only muskets and was about a well-regulated militia. And there's no reference to abortion in the Bible. And other religious traditions have different takes on the actual beginning of "life." These attacks don't work.

Democrats make a big point of hypocrisy. Life is precious before you're born but not after. After that, it's everyone for themselves. As allegedly crooked Texas AG Ken Paxton stated, "the Uvalde shooting was God's will and a message that "life is short." He said this. About dead children. Here's the thing: if Texans don't like it when coastal elites mock them for being dumb rednecks, then stop acting like dumb rednecks. But you can't reason people out of their fears, talk them out of their prejudices, or shake them out of their religious upbringing.

NINE. SEIZE THE MOMENT.

The enormity of the crime of January 6th should have been met with an immediate response. Indictments. Arrests. Not just of the chimps on the ground. Of the planners. The Nazi High Command at the Willard Hotel. And Trump.

Time has washed away the gravity of the crime. It

makes people feel that if it was really that bad, the DOJ would've acted immediately. And since it took so long to act, how bad could it really have been. No matter how many low level goons were tossed in jail, they were the expendables. And we may never see Trump's trial for the biggest crime in the history of the country. Trump understands his play is to delay. If a Democrat is elected, he'll continue to stall. Or flee the country. If he's elected, he'll wipe them all away.

TEN. FUCK THE POLLS. RUN LIKE YOU'RE TEN POINTS DOWN.

Don't call Trump a dictator or authoritarian. That means he's powerful, which is what draws them to him. Power isn't an insult. It's the attraction. Trump's power is their power. What Democrats perceive are his faults, to his supporters are his strengths. The more defiant he is, the more empowered they feel. He's convinced them that his trials are really aimed at them.

Stop playing defense and go on offense. Their mission should be simple: Destroy Donald Trump, politically. Cut the head off the snake and break the spell. There is no replacement. Not one of the MAGA poseurs, including Dollar Store Trump, Ron DeSantis could summon the same loyalty and devotion.

Convict him of all his crimes in the minds of voters. Show how weak and stupid he looks. All it takes is one pinprick to pop this balloon. It's the Wizard of Oz moment. Hit his stupidity. His vanity. His manhood. Rattle him and make him crack so that he folds in the eyes of his adoring sycophants. Mock him in TV spots. Get to the core of their love for him. Make them feel foolish and embarrassed for supporting him. Demean him in front of the faithful. Pull his pants down in public. Make him lose his shit so he disintegrates in public. Goad him. Show him up for being dumb, fat, feeble, deranged. Attack. Demean. Insult. Re-brand him. Hire cult deprogrammers to break the spell.

If third party candidates are the problem, take them out as well. No one attacked Jill Stein in 2016 and she handed us

Trump. Now she's back. Along with Robert F. Kennedy, and Cornel West. And even Marianne Williamson tried to make a comeback, thinking the post-debate fallout opened a lane for her.

I recently heard some Trump flunkie on a local L.A. news station being interviewed in the standard Q and A as he ran through his reasons for putting all power in the hands of the executive branch, Trump's plan if he wins in 2024. And he's been backed up by SCOTUS and given a battle plan with the Heritage Foundation.

This is not just a system test. We are fighting for our lives. Not just our political lives. Our actual lives. Our way of life. They've already taken over the Supreme Court, gotten rid of Roe v Wade, fucked with our voting rights, and gerrymandered congressional districts. And even when they rule that a state like Alabama has to redraw their maps so that they have two Black congressional districts, and fair representation, Alabama says no. They are using democracy to destroy democracy.

Democrats' weakness is their heartfelt belief in the American myth. That might doesn't make right. That goodness always triumphs over evil. That we are fundamentally good, honest people, who will do the right thing, despite Churchill's line about Americans always doing the right thing after they've considered every other possibility. That elections are about policy, or even personality. That there is order underneath the chaos.

We cling to our traditional values and the old rules because they make us feel safe while the ground continues to shift under our feet. Like people in an earthquake trying to hold onto the doorframe, forgetting that everything they could possibly hold onto is also shaking.

Democrats need to learn that you can't drag Trump up to the moral high ground and attack his character, his hypocrisy, and his sins. You have to go down into the low ground valley and beat the political shit out of him.

# CHAPTER FIVE

# WHAT THE MEDIA STILL SCREWS UP

Trump is a five-year-old who walks into a room and scribbles on the wall with his own shit. And the media analyzes the paintings.

In 2012, when he was touting his racist Obama "birther" lie, he was given airtime on CBS, CNN, and The View, along with other shows, with interviewers accepting the basic premise of the lie and asking, "So, what proof do you have that Barack Obama wasn't born in the United States?" That was their first mistake. Putting him on their shows and asking him these question gave him a platform and legitimized the lie.

At that time he was teasing a White House run, and on a stop in the Northeast, his plane was met with a gaggle of reporters. When asked about his allegation, he said, "We have people on the ground [in Hawaii} and they can't believe what they are finding." No one asked "what people?" "What are they finding?" Twelve years later it's clear they found nothing because there never were any people on the ground. It was a Trump-style lie but the media hadn't caught up to his tactics. And they still haven't.

In 2016 the cable news media gave Trump an estimated $3 billion in-kind contribution by airing his rallies in their entirety. Some made the argument that they should show him as he is and let the American people decide. No. Broadcasting those rallies gave him credibility as a candidate he didn't deserve. They should have aired a ten-second clip under the headline: "Deranged, racist maniac loose in local arena."

But the more they put him on TV, the more he gave them. They wanted eyeballs and he knew that if he gave them a crazy or violent clip, people would tune in. That lead to the expectation that every rally would have one of those moments, so they'd tune in for more. To cable news media, these sound bites were ratings heroin.

Then, under the heading of fairness, they booked the Trumpsplainers on their shows, allowing them to bulldoze the truth to a draw, further legitimizing an illegitimate candidate. The worst of them was, and still is, Kellyanne Conway, who rescued Trump's campaign when he was alienating women by referring to them as pigs, and saying they should be punished for having abortions.

When he staged his birther walk-back "press conference" in 2016, right before the first debate, the media showed up en masse, some even training their cameras on an empty podium in anticipation of his arrival. One or two discontinued the feed as they began to realize they were being played.

Even dating back to the '80s in New York, Trump knew how to play the media. Now, the game has changed. There is no media. There is a fragmented news/opinion landscape with a myriad of platforms and delivery systems. Network, cable, streaming, video, the podcast multi-verse, social media. The term "news" itself is almost an anachronism. Once upon a time, it implied the delivery of facts from a trusted source whose only goal was to communicate information, whether they knew it or were in the process of finding it out. If there was confusion, they said there was confusion. If there was a difference of opinion, they cited that as well.

The days of the Big Three networks, as trusted go-to news sources are gone. Even *The New York Times, Washington Post*, and *Wall Street Journal* are not pure. CNN, and MSNBC are corporate entities and, as such, have always been in a push-pull between holding to journalistic principles of fairness and objectivity while fighting for viewers. Is there ever a story that's not "breaking news?"

Fox News jumped on the cable train but managed to build a pseudo-news channel, creating a Frankenstein monster out of the look of a traditional news source, combined with the bad intent of Soviet propaganda. They call it news when it fits the moment, and opinion when they have to deflect blowback from a lie, or from presenting fantasy as fact. Even a $787 million judgment for defamation hasn't pushed them off their business model.

Fox went so far as to put a psychic tarot card reader on the air, who regrettably, for them, predicted Trump's demise.

Even erstwhile golden boy Tucker Carlson tried to fight his way back to relevancy by interviewing Putin, which was actually less an interview than a Lauren Boebert theater date. Fox continues to pump out its brand of bombastic intellectual sewage, though their shtick now seems almost quaint by current standards.

Their "alternative news" model has been taken up by Newsmax, Sinclair, and OANN. There's X/Twitter, which is a virtual thermometer up the ass of the American public, with a sidebar of Russian bots. Combo Bond villain and Golum imitator, Emo Skum, put his imprimatur on the site, dragging it down into an info/opinion hellscape, as competitors spring up almost daily. Substacks, websites, YouTube channels, Bloomberg News, Puck, The Daily Beast, Joe Rogan. 4chan, 8chan, Reddit, Facebook. Tiktok. Post, Discord, Mastodon, Tribel, CounterSocial, Sproutible. Trump's feeble Truth Social. We're fighting out our future online waiting to see who gets the last LOL.

Even comedy shows are in the mix. The Daily Show, once again featuring Jon Stewart. Bill Maher. Jon Oliver. These shows have provided a comedic counterpoint to stories aired on traditional media, and occasionally even more facts and context than those traditional sources.

While the cable news outlets finally realized how they got played in 2016, some have moderately corrected. In 2024, as we may be stumbling our way toward dictatorship, some sound the fascist alarm, rising above the day to day noise to point out that these are dangerous times and Trump is a dangerous person. And, yet, they still occasionally get played, or even play themselves. These are five mistakes I continue to see.

ONE: NEVER GIVE TRUMP A PLATFORM

In his 1964 book, "Understanding Media: The Extensions of Man, Marshall McLuhan coined the phrase "The medium is the message." The meaning: it's not just the content of what's being communicated, it's the forum in which it's set." Every picture tells a story.

Trump is the Republican candidate so he must be reported on. And, as he rarely gives interviews to those he calls "the fake news," when he agrees to it, he's just using it. He knows how to play the media. He knows how to control it. One way is through the setting of the traditional interview, which is never a real interview in the sense of questions, answers, and follow-up questions. It's not an exchange of ideas or debates on policy. It's a phenomenon that exists somewhere between a photo op and a crime scene. For Trump, it's an opportunity to use the traditional visual of the interview or town hall to firehose his way through questions so that it ends up being an infomercial. It also presents the moment as one in which he overpowers the interviewer, which empowers him with his supporters. And in those few moments where he appears normal, it opens a door for undecided voters to consider him. But, most often, his goal is to dominate by taking advantage of the host's dedication to fairness.

Trump doesn't respond to questions, he reacts to them. He forces his dominance in the conversation like the interviewer was in a dressing room at Bergdorf Goodman. If the host attempts a follow-up question or disputes his account he cuts them off with "Excuse me! Excuse me!" He shoots down attacks like he's got an iron dome over him. He knows it's about strength and weakness, not the specifics of the issue. He steamrolls his way through the moment, lying his gargantuan ass off and overpowering the poor interviewer. If he's ignorant about a subject or doesn't want to commit to anything he says, "we're looking at this" or "we're going to announce a policy in two weeks." This makes him seem like he knows what he's talking about yet keeps him non-committal, and immune to rebuttal, while masking his true ignorance. He knows no one will ever follow up so he can successfully play for time. It's the illusion of a response. Basic Trump logorrhea.

He uses the forum for its PR value to come off like an actual candidate. The forum itself gives him credibility. If you give him an interview, he's already won. Still media outlets keep staging and promoting these events thinking that honest questions and tough-sounding follow-ups will somehow pin him down. They book him on their shows as a ratings stunt not realizing that the event has nothing to do with journalism.

Even Jonathan Swan, who sat down with him in August of 2020 and was aggressive in his questioning, may have momentarily thrown Trump off his game but he didn't ultimately "take him down" as many reports claimed.

In May, 2023 CNN gave Trump a town hall that he blasted his way through, bulldozing the moderator, Kaitlin Collins. Same mistake. They also allowed him to stock the audience with supporters who laughed at his dumb, cruel jokes and applauded at the right times. Giving him that photo-op forfeited context because it allowed him to portray himself as a legitimate candidate, which is now an even more dangerous phenomenon than in 2016 or 2020.

MSNBC made the identical mistake in their September, 2023 re-launch of *Meet The Press* with Kristen Welker by giving Trump a sit-down interview. Same picture. Same results.

Trump's acolytes also play the same game. In their 2023 series finale Showtime's *The Circus* interviewed Steve Bannon and let him spew his insane bullshit without countering him by smashing him in the face with a baseball bat. Smiles, smirks, knowing glances or cutaways couldn't erase the shit coming from his porcine mouth. It wasn't even a ratings stunt because they'd been cancelled. The premise of allowing him spew his lies, and letting the public to make up its own mind didn't play. Giving him the forum afforded him a legitimacy they couldn't take back.

In November, 2023, *60 Minutes* interviewed John Eastman, the now disbarred former dean at the Chapman University Law School (where, coincidentally, I'm writing this. Not the law school, the campus). Eastman is the frog-faced, right wing maniac who devised the "legal" blueprint for the January 6th attack. Instead of being arrested, he was given airtime on a major news program. And while the interviewer asked a few follow-up questions, Eastman was not exposed as a traitor, and the lies went out, unchallenged.

My fear is that this practice will only get worse as we get closer to the election, when access becomes more important. It's not a matter of ignoring him. Obviously, he's not going away. The question is, how do you report what he says and does while putting it in the proper context.

Trump's intentions are to gain power in order to destroy Democracy. This is a new phenomenon in American politics and can't be dealt with by the standards and practices of traditional journalism.

TWO. DON'T TRY TO DISPROVE TRUMP'S LIES BY STATING, "THERE'S NO PROOF OF THE LIE."

The response to the allegation "The 2020 election was stolen" should never have been: "There's no proof that the 2020 election was stolen." Repeating the lie in order to deny it allows the lie to Trojan Horse its way into the public debate. What hangs in the air, like a fart in an oxygen tank, are the words.... "The 2020 election was stolen."

Trump is a bank robber who bursts through the doors, shoots his gun in the air, and screams, "Everybody hit the floor! Put the money in the bags!" Then, on the way out, he stares into the security camera and screams: "The tellers robbed the bank!" Then he runs out and the cops don't chase him for two years.

And even though it's all on closed circuit video and it's clearly him holding the gun, the Justice Department needs to investigate the matter, as Trump continues to scream that it's all fake news, there was no robbery, and if there was, it was the tellers who robbed the bank.

Then Fox and right wing media pick up the story by flogging the actions of the crooked tellers while the "woke" media tackles both sides of the teller "controversy" by bringing on a panel of experts to debate it, while breaking down the video frame by frame like it was the Zapruder film. Then Trump holds interviews and claims that the video was a deep fake, and he never robbed the bank and even if he did he's got millions if not billions in that bank and would have every right to rob it if he wanted to but he didn't because, as everyone knows, the crooked tellers robbed the bank and should be investigated. And when the interviewer notes that Trump has been spending the stolen money and that the serial numbers on the bills are a perfect match, and his fingerprints are everywhere, he cries that the deep state is trying to frame him, and "the government prints the money so they are part of the conspiracy."

Then the media responds by saying there is "no evidence that the tellers robbed the bank." They show the footage of Trump robbing the bank, which he continues to call "deep fakes," as he's just recently learned the expression and it makes him feel smart to use it. He once again blames the crooked tellers. Then the FBI investigates the tellers and discovers that one of them had her car repossessed and has credit problems. The next night, the lead news story is "Teller-gate!" Reporters and camera crews camp outside the teller's home, shoving microphones and cameras in their face, asking if they were responsible for the robbery.

Then the Justice Department spends two years investigating and building a case, before hiring a Special Prosecutor, who eventually issues indictments. They trace the money he spent to the stolen money from the bank, and Trump claims the FBI, the Treasury, and the entire deep state conspired to frame him. Then trial dates are set, which he stalls with an endless stream of motions stating that he didn't rob the bank, but he had a right to rob the bank because some of his money was in there, and the money was returned to the economy by spending it so it was a victimless crime, and former presidents are technically allowed to rob banks because whatever they do while in office is protected by presidential immunity.

Then he goes on trial for a different crime, which the media covers gavel-to-gavel, interviewing legal experts, while Trump insults and even threatens the judge, the judge's family and the jury, and when he's ordered to shut up or pay a fine he engages an endless stream of sycophantic congressional surrogates to show up outside the courtroom in matching outfits to demean the judge, the jury, and the legal system, and parrot his bullshit talking points as a loyalty test and/or a Vice Presidential audition. Then he's convicted, and appeals. And it all comes off as a summer stock production of *And Justice For All.* "You're out of order! The whole system's out of order!"

The media needs to put the lies in the proper context. This is Soviet-era, Russian-style propaganda, disinformation and manipulation and we don't have a history of it. We haven't grown up in it enough to develop that layer of cynicism. We're not thinkers. We're not skeptics. Or cynics. That takes too much energy. We're a nation of believers. Always yearning for something to believe in. And because of that, we're easily fooled.

THREE. LEGAL ANALYSIS WITHOUT REALPOLITIK CONTEXT IS JUST BLOVIATING.

Legal scholars, and expert analysts have fulfilled an important role in explaining the intricacies of the law, and the legal system. How it should function. And how it can be manipulated.

Cable news has an all-star team of lawyers and constitutional scholars, like Neil Katyal, Andrew Weismann, J. Michael Luttig, Joyce Vance, and Lawrence Tribe, who started out clearly explaining the law to viewers though occasionally seems so beaten down by the daily insanity that I sometimes expect him to throw up his hands and go full "fuck this guy." Yes, they do explain the law, though, at times, there's too much information and analysis and not enough realpolitik.

One night on Lawrence O'Donnell's show the subject was the 14th Amendment and whether Trump should be allowed to run for president after fomenting an insurrection against the United States. One pundit was a law school professor who was so giddy at the prospect of schooling the public on the history and philosophical foundation of the 14th Amendment that he went on for at least ten minutes, vomiting up a torrent of history and facts. It was literal TMI. And the host was unable to cut him off. It was painful, even borderline insufferable. Just a pedant getting high on his own supply without adding any real world context. He was making arguments that would convince no one and, in fact, piss off nearly everyone sitting in my dining room. At one point even I was screaming at the TV for this egghead to shut the fuck up. In that moment, I understood why they hate us. It reminded me of a Woody Allen line about intellectuals being brilliant, and yet having no idea what's going on.

The question in the air has always been what the Supreme Court would do. Even if every single justice agreed with his historical and legal analysis and concurred that, based on Trump's actions and the original intent of the amendment, he should be kept off the ballot (in this case it was the Colorado ballot), this Court, given its ideological configuration, was never going to do that. Some were already on his side. Others feared the backlash.

You may have a sublime legal, historical or philosophical argument but the only real takeaway from this case is what is likely to happen. As well, to pretend that we're dealing with a pure analysis of the law and not politics is to be dangerously naïve.

We were in the same world with the presidential immunity case. They'd already stalled the Jan. 6 trial by taking the case. And they're all intimately aware of the power of time. They put their finger on the scale for Trump by blocking that trial during an election year. People waited to see if they would rule and they finally did, giving Trump even more immunity, amounting to a tacit endorsement of treason, and a lifetime get out of jail free card. So much for Ginni Thomas' text messages and Alito's wife's upside-down flags.

FOUR: STOP GAMING OUT THE HORSERACE.

In October 2023, an episode of Showtime's *The Circus* was centered on the GOP primaries in Iowa and New Hampshire. Despite the fact that it was a foregone conclusion that Trump would get the nomination, it was all horserace, all the time. Who's up? Who's down? Who's got momentum? Will DeSantis out-MAGA Trump? Is Vivek the Republican Obama? Will Chris Christie find a lane and gain traction? Can Nikki Haley escape from the pack? Even though there was no real race, the events took place so they had to be reported on. But what should have been the appropriate context?

Had they been around during the revolution and Paul Revere's ride they'd be discussing which British were coming, and from what direction, and wearing what color uniforms and what type of muskets are they holding and how far they can shoot and why do they march in lockstep.

Without providing context, which is that everyone on that stage represented a dangerous trend in their party, let alone the country, the reporting was the political equivalent of covering the Westminster Dog Show.

FIVE: DON'T GLOAT. DON'T BOTH-SIDES EVERYTHING. FUCK FAIRNESS.

In March, 2017 there was great buzz over a story that was about to be reported by Rachel Maddow that they "got Trump's tax returns." They whipped it up to fever pitch, only to have it turn out to be a couple pages that were leaked, the effect of which was pre-empted and neutered by Trump's White House and Fox News. A "nothing-burger." All hype and no story. Yet, the buzz created in anticipation on par with Geraldo's Rivera's uncovering of Al Capone's vault. In the end, it was meaningless.

The tone of many MSNBC stories has become "we got him now." Yes, the stories are important, and they serve to keep Trump's feet to the fire and expose the lies, but they never deliver a knockout punch. It also feeds the illusion that we're in a world where ideas and truth matter. We're not. That's the battle we're fighting and that world will hopefully be one we return to.

I'll admit these are hard times for legitimate journalists. The truth may not set you free, all by itself. The facts are not always the truth. It's a game of juggling accuracy, and impartiality with the reality of being played by propagandists.

In that world, I say fuck fairness. Fairness is weakness. That was the original sin of 2016. Kellyanne Conway ran rampant over the liberal airwaves as they postured at how even-handed they were. Look at what good journalists we are! We're presenting both sides!

Trump games the system at every turn. Univision not only gave him an interview but canceled Biden's ads in response. New ownership is allied with Trump as he makes further inroads into Hispanic voters. Dems have been losing this base since 2016. Getting Univision on his side is like getting Spanish Fox. This is huge and can't be underestimated.

In March, 2024 MSNBC momentarily hired Ronna Romney McDaniel, former head of the RNC. The one who referred to January 6th as a tourist visit. There is nothing else to know about their agenda. Yes, she was ultimately un-hired but the hiring itself was a dangerous concession. Not to fairness, but to lust for viewership.

It is the media's job to inform the American public. This means not giving legitimate interviews to people saying illegitimate things. You don't bend over for the person who's trying to pick your pocket.

The public, unfortunately, is not equipped to simply make up its own mind. "We report, you decide." We're not taught how to recognize propaganda. We're not schooled to be skeptics. We're not thinkers. We're believers. And we've been told that all of our opinions and beliefs are equally valid because we're allowed to have them.

The technique of wading into a Trump rally with a camera and microphone and asking people simple questions in the hope of getting an idiotic answer, as the host turns a side eye to camera, suggesting that their stupidity is self-evident, is not the game changer it may once have been.

The job of the media during an attack is not to report the attacker's point of view in an effort to present both sides. It's not to game out the success rate of the attacker and how they're doing in the polls.

The challenge becomes how to practice responsible

journalism when one side is using your sense of responsibility to play you, and, if successful, possibly even destroy you. When fascism is trying to beat down the door is traditional objectivity a valid stance? If you are standing outside a burning building is it your job to report that there appears to be some smoke, flames, and intense heat emanating from the location, or do you scream "fire!" Do you just hang out with your crew waiting to interview the firefighters, calibrating whether the level of water pressure will be enough to put out the fire, and how long that might take. And how tall are the ladders? And how tall are the firefighters? And have they made a calendar? And what do you do about the lunatic on the corner holding a gas can and box of matches who insists there's no fire and that it's all a hoax. Especially if that lunatic is a member of Congress. Or a former president.

# CHAPTER SIX

# REALITY WARS

# BREAKING DOWN OUR FUNDAMENTAL PHILOSOPHICAL DISCONNECT

*Exodus 32. When the people saw that Moses was so long in coming down from the mountain, they gathered around Aaron and said, "come, make us gods" who will go before us… Aaron answered them, "Take off your gold earrings and bring them to me… He took what they handed him and made it into an idol cast in the shape of a calf. He said, "Tomorrow there will be a festival to the lord. So the next day the people sacrificed burnt offerings and afterward they sat down to eat and drink and got up to indulge in revelry…"*

This is where we are in America. Drowning in our worship of false gods. The gods of fame, money, excess, ignorance, guns, and pride in stupidity. The Kardashians went from a joke to a business model. Reality TV became TV. Social media influencer, YouTube star, and TikTok famous became real things. And they all congealed into a giant malignant mass in Donald Trump. He is our golden calf. Unfortunately, way too many of us are still dancing around it and there's no Moses to come down from the mountain to bust up the party.

We used to be a United States. Well, since 1789, with a temporary separation from 1861-1865, but then we got back together, albeit with legal segregation and confederate statues. But at least we went back to agreeing on the basics. Not any more. Now, we barely agree on anything. We don't agree on life, liberty, or the definition of happiness, let alone the pursuit of it. We can't even agree on sitting down and discussing it. And even if we could agree, we don't know how. We've blasted past "let's talk it out" to "let's fight it out."

Any philosophical argument has to begin with a definition of terms, which forces one back to first principles, which are occasionally unreflectively held value systems based on a set of beliefs. They're either beliefs one inherited, learned, or was indoctrinated into. We don't engage in those discussions. One side is too dumb, angry and aggrieved. The other side is too long-winded, pedantic, and moralistic.

We're just not a philosophical people. We're not trained to think. We don't have thoughts. We have beliefs. And we're told that our beliefs are sacrosanct, based on the fact that we believe them. "We no longer agree on good faith dialogue as a means for problem solving. "Well, that's what I believe" has become the ultimate argument ender regardless of whether that opinion has any basis in fact. We've conflated everyone's right to their beliefs and opinions with the validity of those beliefs and opinions. The juvenile level of our public debate has lowered the intellectual bar, so that even fantasy-based arguments now fall within a legitimate range of ideas. We've slipped into a world where some question basic scientific fact and expertise. Hence: the anti-vax movement.

I seriously doubt that if one of these self-described anti-vax medical skeptics had a heart attack and was rushed to the ER and, after the basic tests, was told that they had blockages in multiple arteries and needed immediate bypass surgery that they would say, "Hold on, 'Doctor'. Before you start cutting based on your medical "expertise," I want to consult a naturopath, an osteopath, a chiropractor, an herbalist, an acupuncturist, a holistic healer, a dietician, a shaman, a radio show host, and some rando high school dropout in a small town diner."

You don't have to have blind faith in modern medicine or absolute trust in the beneficent nature of Big Pharma to accept that a deadly virus can hurt or kill you, and that it makes sense to do everything in your power to protect yourself. Pharmaceutical companies have gouged the fuck out of people who need certain drugs to survive but they've also come up with those very life-saving drugs. There's a difference between healthy skepticism of medical experts, and negating medical science out of hand because you're mad at a virus for screwing up your life.

We may not all be rocket scientists but, up until recently, we had no fundamental disagreement over the truth of rocket science, particularly when you could launch a satellite into space, have it collect data, and then return back to Earth.

The fault ultimately lies in our education system. We're not taught how to engage in philosophical argument. We're so busy screaming at or lecturing each other, trying to prove our points or beat the opposition into submission that we never dig down to the root of our disagreements to reveal the underlying assumptions and whether they're uncritically held or even based in reality.

We get attached to the myths and stories we're fed as children and they become the basis of our thoughts, values, and identities. And because of that we tend to cling to those ideas. To surrender, or even open then up to discussion can lead one to feel vulnerable, or even attacked. Most people don't like it when you shake the ground under their feet. The more you challenge someone's core beliefs, the more you'll be met with anger and, sometimes, bullets.

And at the root of our American disconnect is a fundamental misunderstanding about the nature and purpose of religion.

## AMERICA HAS A RELIGION PROBLEM

It's said that there are two things you don't talk to strangers about: politics and religion. And because this subject is so loaded it rarely gets discussed in a public forum with any depth.

For the most part we accept gravity, aerodynamics, photosynthesis, relativity, quantum mechanics, sexual reproduction, rain, thunder, earthquakes, volcanoes and tidal waves all based on science. But when it comes to the origin and nature of life itself we take leave of our senses for a trip into the supernatural. We quite literally lose our minds.

Even though the Library of Congress houses over 38 million books, in 470 languages, on 530 miles of bookshelves, we're told that the truth of human existence can be found in a literal interpretation of one of several centuries-old books of dubious authorship that are riddled with myth, prejudice, and superstition. And no one questions it.

Despite advancements in medicine, we still light candles, engage in prayer circles, travel to Lourdes for magic healing waters, and get on our knees and pray to a statue in the hope that it can cure us.

We've confused freedom of religion with the notion that any behavior or statement, no matter how idiotic, carries an inherent legitimacy as long as it's grounded in a person's faith. Chronologically this may be the 21st century, but intellectually it's the Dark Ages.

When it comes to religion, we don't understand the original intent behind the phenomenon so we're lost in an endless loop of anthropomorphic gods, ghost stories, silly beliefs, and a mindless obedience to customs and rituals. Or the outright rejection of anything falling under the heading of religion as total and complete nonsense.

We've accepted this notion of "religious differences," which could be translated into "the things I do to be more in touch with life and be a kinder, gentler, more compassionate person are better than the things you do to be more in touch with life and be a kinder, gentler, more compassionate person. So, I'm going to have to kill you."

It's our club vs. theirs. Our building vs. theirs. Our clothes vs. theirs. Our book vs. theirs. Our customs vs. theirs. Our homeland vs. theirs. And it's posed as a zero sum game. Only one can be right, therefore everyone else's is wrong.

We've inherited a broken paradigm for discussing religion that runs through four categories:

1) You're a believer. You believe in the Old Testament Sky Daddy God as both universe creator and moralist in chief. You believe everything in the dusty old books is literally true, since it was dictated by God and is therefore sacred so everyone must live according to the specific dictates in those books. You reject science and reason as the methods for discovering the origin and nature of life and the physical universe. And anyone who doesn't agree with your beliefs or in any way challenges them is a heretic who should be shunned, silenced, or killed.

2) You're an atheist, proudly proclaiming, "I'm too smart to believe any of that stupid shit. I can make sense of the world and my life based solely on reason and observable fact. Religion, by any definition, is just a collection of ghost stories. A personal choice when it shapes the way someone leads their own life, but a dangerous intrusion when those people cross the line by trying to tell me how to live mine. I don't need the ghost stories to make sense of life in general, my life, specifically, or ground my sense of morality."

3) You're an agnostic, exclaiming, "Maybe there's a God, maybe there isn't. It's all too vast for we mortals to know."

4) Finally, there's the "Well, I'm not traditionally religious but I'm very spiritual," crowd. Essentially this means you eat vegan and drive a Tesla to hot yoga. Most people don't hear the arrogance underlying this pronouncement, which is actually antithetical to the goal of religious practice. There's also the pantheistic group that celebrates all things "interfaith" and applauds when the people from the different

groups get along even though that is exactly what religious people are supposed to do.

This is the philosophical framework we've inherited for understanding and discussing religion, and it's not only wrong, but dangerous, and is at the core of our basic differences in this country. We don't understand the true nature of religion and why it's existed, in any form, over the millennia. We don't think it's a subject that can be discussed. And even when we try we don't have the tools or the language. We don't teach religion in schools. Not indoctrination into a specific tradition but the history and philosophy underlying all traditions, even though, in many cases, they have been perverted out of all recognition.

The word "religion" itself comes from the Latin *re-ligio*, meaning, in this case, to re-connect with an experience of universality. Religion has nothing to do with the origin of the physical universe. That is a matter for science. Religion also has nothing to do with sex.

It's not about religious belief. It's about religious practice, and rituals that are meant to take us out of our usual personal pursuits to focus on a direct experience of our commonality. In Freudian terms, it's about less Id, and more Super-ego. Prayer, and meditation are activities that are meant to clear the mind, open the heart, soften the spirit, and move one toward a less ego-based experience of life. Sadly, most Americans remain tragically ignorant of this. And this fundamental ignorance infects almost all aspects of our lives.

The notion of "religious differences" is no more fundamental than food differences, art differences, music differences, or fashion differences. Different traditions have different customs, practices, art, symbols, and rituals, all designed for the same exact purpose: to guide someone toward a more universal experience of life. As such, it has nothing to do with the origin of the physical universe. And it has nothing to do with sex.

## BECAUSE WE HAVE A RELIGION PROBLEM
## WE HAVE A SEX PROBLEM

Sex is human reproduction. It's basic biology. There's nothing religious, moral or immoral about it. If you believe there's a God who created everything then that God created sex, and if you have a problem with that you should take it up with the manufacturer. And if you do, you can enquire about the fact that an omniscient being who created all things made a core mistake in how we replicate and therefore had to issue a book to clarify His original intentions. So much for omniscience.

Sex feels good. If it didn't feel good, there'd be eight people on Earth. Religious obsession with sex is the result of a literal devotion to a book filled with ignorance, prejudices and misogyny that was written by a bunch of camel-fuckers who lived in deserts halfway around the world, thousands of years ago.

We've also been told that this sky daddy God believes that sex is reserved only for marriage. Another divine screw-up. If God intended sex to be exclusively reserved for marriage, then even if you believe that the Earth is only 6000 years old, but accept that the institution of marriage is only 4000 years old, then for 2000 years there was a whole lot of illegitimate fucking going on. And right under God's nose. Was this just an oversight?

Religion has nothing to do with sex. And sex has nothing to do with shame or sin. The Garden of Eden is not a lesson on the evils of nudity. The fall from grace is about straying from a universal experience of life -- a direct experience of the fundamental unity with all things. Not an intellectual acceptance of that fact, but an experience of it.

Being "religious" has been perverted into being some sort of sexual prig, and has lead to a strain of misogyny that has infected our customs, our laws, and our lives, specifically our argument over abortion.

## BECAUSE WE HAVE A RELIGION PROBLEM
## WE HAVE AN ABORTION PROBLEM

Women get pregnant. Last I heard, men had something to do with it, but women have to bear the burden. That's biology. Again, if you think that's s a problem, take it up with the boss. As mentioned, we're not a philosophical people, so we can't seem to rationally engage in this discussion in the public sphere.

No one is pro-abortion. No 16-year-old thinks, "I'm pregnant and my boyfriend is ghosting me and my parents are going to kill me but at least, on the upside, I get to have an abortion." And no one is doing capricious late-term abortions. No one carries a baby to term, then wakes up one morning and thinks, "Nah. Never mind. Let's kill it." The only late-term abortion would be if the kid came out with its hands up, screaming: "Please, don't abort me!"

So, let's just lay the arguments out. As a basic premise I agree with the intention behind the idea that life is sacred. In general, respecting life is a more civilized approach, and leads to more beneficent human behavior. And since a fertilized egg is, in the broadest sense, alive and can potentially grow into a person, I understand the passion of some people who are anti-abortion, because it comes from a basically noble place. Of course, many of those same people fail to demonstrate that same reverence for all life outside of the womb. They love embryos. Actual children -- not so much. But that's a secondary argument. I also think that in the past there's been a casualness to abortion that belied the emotional reality.

The primary argument against abortion is that it is taking a life. That it's technically murder. But that is based on one's definition of when life "begins" and this is where the trouble starts. This is where reverence for life runs into primitive attitudes about sex, along with Biblical misogyny.

Religious people claim that life "begins" at conception. That an embryo is a person. That it's God's baby and that a woman is nothing more than an incubator. The most extreme believe that it doesn't matter if that embryo was the result of rape or incest. Once conceived, it is a living thing. I understand the emotion. But since we don't live in a theocracy those feelings shouldn't rule our lives, when most people don't share them. These are tough choices, like the death penalty. Or war. Each of which involves killing.

As much as the anti-abortion side thinks they are defending an objective fact; they're not. They feel they are acting with absolute moral authority. But even when you pass a 6-week abortion ban, as draconian as that is, then your absolutist argument goes out the window because you've accepted the notion that there is a window between conception and person-hood.

Sure, if you look at the series of pictures of fetal development it certainly feels like at some point the embryo has developed to some stage of personhood. So, to discuss abortion one has to accept that it is based on a value judgment centered around the determination of when life "begins." You cannot establish an absolute beginning of life as it's not an objective fact. Science can provide guidance as to the development, experience, and viability of the fetus. The protections once afforded by Roe v. Wade were based on fetal viability outside the womb, which is usually between 24 and 28 weeks.

Once you accept that there is a decision to be made about the number of weeks involved then you've accepted that this is a society's choice. Which means it's an individual's choice. And since women get pregnant, it's a woman's choice. And it's a right that can't be taken away. And that is the next part of the argument.

Government can't assert that a woman has civil rights until she gets pregnant, at which point those rights revert to the state. Pregnancy doesn't turn a woman from a citizen into an incubator. That's not only not religious; it's anti-American. Why does the moniker "right to life" apply to a fetus more than the woman who's carrying it? Why should a person lose their right to life, liberty and the pursuit of happiness simply because they get pregnant?

Abortion is a medical procedure. From a health care point of view, abortion is a private transaction between a woman and her doctor. Like any other medical decision anyone else makes about anything having to do with their body. As such it's no one else's business. Not the federal government. Not state government. Not local government. Not any government. If her boyfriend, husband, or parents become part of that equation then that is her choice. It shouldn't even have to be said. It's even patronizing (interesting word, etymologically) for men to come out and declare that it's a woman's right to choose. At this point women should rise up and tell men who are trying to take away their human rights that they should, in every sense of the expression, go fuck themselves.

No one can be denied a medical procedure that they and their doctor decide is desirable or necessary. No one would be denied an appendectomy, heart transplant, vasectomy, or Tommy John surgery. If some guy had a torn meniscus and his doctor recommended arthroscopic knee surgery but then a counsel of elder women barged in and declared that they forbid him to have knee surgery based on their belief that the man's knee injury was God's intention and no human has the right to intervene, there would be a strong reaction. But what happens if he has the surgery and then he and his entire surgical team are arrested? That's where we're headed.

We have the ability to perform abortions safely and that option has become a part of our lives and basic health care. Republicans may be enjoying the end of Roe v. Wade, while laying in wait to enact even more primitive laws not just about abortion but about sex, contraception, and marriage. But if they take power, here's what's going to happen as a result. All women are going to suffer. Including Republican women. As well as the men in their lives. Because biology and anatomy don't recognize political affiliation. Republican women are going to have ectopic pregnancies, fetal abnormalities, and a host of other complications because that's just basic reproductive reality. There will be teenage pregnancies. There will be pregnancies resulting from rape and incest. These things will happen. These things are happening.

So, let's see what happens when it's the wives, girlfriends, and daughters of Republican men who begin to suffer. How many of them will be content to bleed out in a car in a hospital parking lot because they've been denied necessary medical care.

Women are being denied a medical procedure based on the "religious" beliefs of a minority, albeit one that has gained power on the Supreme Court. This is discrimination. This is a privacy issue. It's a civil rights issue. It's also a commerce issue because someone is being denied a service they want and can afford.

So what we're left with is medicine's ability to perform safe abortions and the concept of when life "begins." Which is a value judgment. You can namedrop God and the Bible all you want, but in a free society if most people don't agree with your argument, then your religious feelings don't get to rule the day.

We have separation of church and state. Religious beliefs, however passionate, are just that – beliefs. And while they can be the personal reason one doesn't get an abortion, no one has the right to determine how other people live, otherwise that religious minority's beliefs would govern every area of our lives. And we don't live in a theocracy. Yet.

## BECAUSE WE HAVE A RELIGION PROBLEM
## WE HAVE AN LGBTQ PROBLEM

Over the years, we've matured as a society, going from the closeted '50s to the liberated "60s and '70s, through the Don't Ask Don't Tell '80s, through AIDS, to Obergefell, and now the Secretary of Transportation is a Harvard educated, Rhodes scholar, gay-married war veteran with kids. That's a pretty cool resume no matter which side you're on. If we have a democratic future in this country, he's it. If. But the whole trans rights thing is reigniting those old conflicting feelings and now Republicans are freaking out and are obsessed with slamming everyone back into the closet.

Liberation movements have simultaneously freed some people and frightened others. Every movement for social change has run head first into reactionaries. People are scared of change because they are scared of the unknown or of what they know about themselves and are conflicted about revealing. Republicans flogged the fear of gay marriage in Ohio in 2004 and it won Bush the election. They know how to push those buttons.

Most people are born with hormones and body parts that sync up with their feelings. But not all people. There's a balance of male and female in all of us. But in some that balance shifts and people simply respond to how they feel inside.

A certain percentage of people will experience sexuality on a continuum and their body parts won't always match up in the traditional fashion with their desires. Even if it's a relatively small percentage, it's a real percentage. And we still don't have the proper language to discuss actual reality. We're locked in a struggle between what is the norm, meaning what is usual, and what is normal, meaning actual human experience. And religion is at the heart of it.

America is stuck in an internal battle between the rules and customs they've been born into and the ability to think themselves out of them when they become restrictive. Even the word "tolerance" has been perverted as it implies acceptance but carries a connotation of some disagreeable thing or person one begrudgingly tolerates. It's not about tolerance. It's about knowledge. Understanding. An awareness of life as it is.

The more sexual fluidity is accepted as part of life the more all people are liberated to live genuine lives. However, people whose minds have been twisted by a damaging religious upbringing will panic, and fight back. Usually with anger, which is fear, or self-loathing turned outward.

That reaction has taken the form of people, usually in red states, becoming terrified that educating their children about the range of human sexuality will somehow indoctrinate them into being gay or romanticize the notion of gender fluidity, despite the fact that no one would go through changing their gender identity and all that entails if they weren't responding to exactly what they felt inside. No parent would ever put their child through that, capriciously.

No one is advocating exposing children to more knowledge than they are ready to take in. You'd think reasonable people could figure that one out. When puberty kicks in, knowledge better come in with it, or you're going to raise a generation of very confused children getting facts off the internet. And it will directly lead to more teenage pregnancies. And to those in Louisiana who made it a law that the Ten Commandments must be displayed in every classroom, how were you planning on explaining the one about adultery?

The more a country's laws and society's customs are in sync with actual human experience, the more it has the right to refer to itself as civilized. And that should be the goal. To lead civilized lives. And that starts with education.

## AMERICA HAS AN
## EDUCATION PROBLEM

Americans tend to define themselves in terms of the work they do. Work and money imply value. You are what you do, what you make and what you have. Based on that notion is the assumption that the nature and purpose of education is vocational training.

Yes, at some point people need to follow their passions or hone their talents to make a living. That's the way we do things here. But the goal of a society should be to create smarter people and more informed citizens, not just more efficient workers. Assuming people who have blue-collar jobs can't be informed politically is the bigotry of low expectations. We can have educated, intellectual plumbers. These are not mutually exclusive categories.

We also have a civics problem. We force students to say the Pledge of Allegiance every morning but we fail to educate them about the history and philosophy of democracy. And how it differs from capitalism. One is a system of government. The other is a system of business and labor. They are separate in theory though intertwined in practice. At times democracy has had to serve as a governor on the abuses of capitalism.

There is also a popular assumption that studying humanities and the arts is elitist, or serves the clandestine intentions of the "radical left." Public education is under attack by forces using the paper tigers of CRT, DEI, and sex education to disguise their real agenda, which is to siphon tax dollars into private; i.e., religious schools. They use the propaganda tool of "school choice" and "vouchers," which sounds fair until you get to their real agenda, which is to starve public schools and channel money and young minds into private parochial schools where they can indoctrinate instead of educate.

One tactic in their efforts is to demonize public education based on lies. I've had four children matriculate through the LAUSD public school system. (Yes, here, in radical L.A.) The teachers, administrators, counselors have all been compassionate, dedicated professionals. And, I assume, underpaid. (You couldn't pay me enough to deal with other people's kids all day long. I can barely deal with my own.)

You know what my kids study? English, math, science, history. PE. Their electives have included mythology, and filmmaking. But not once on drop off has my kid ever been asked to pick a gender. No one stands over them in class demanding that they recognize their White privilege and repent. No one demands they pee in a litter box. No middle school children are being forced to read *Lolita* and write a book report to be delivered to the entire class. It's a lie. It's not happening.

We are also on the verge of another technical revolution with AI. Students must be able to keep up in the world. Unless one goes off the grid and back to nature, it is impossible to live one's life off-line. We have to have one eye on the future but another on the past.

We need to build a society that is intelligent, socially conscious, and moral enough to handle the tools that will be put at our disposal. We need to teach History. Philosophy. Psychology. Ethics. Civics. Whether it's atomic weapons, social media, or AI, we are in danger of growing a generation of business and computer experts, and social and political idiots. Without a fundamental education, the tools we put in their hands will be infinitely more self-destructive.

# AMERICA
# HAS A
# GOVERNMENT
# PROBLEM

Back in the '80s, Republican saint Ronald Reagan quipped: "The nine most terrifying words in the English language are 'I'm from the government and I'm here to help'." Frankly, those were the eighteen most terrifying words, as they cast doubt on the idea of government itself. Also implied in his comment was the sanctification of wealth and the holiness of the invisible hand of the market, with all its religious overtones. It also conveyed the idea that money is, in and of itself, holy, however it's accrued. It's not surprising that a famous movie quote from that decade was: "Greed is Good."

Underlying this notion is a fallacy about the role and purpose of government. Particularly democratic government. Government is not a business, nor should it be run like one. It's not meant to turn a profit. Business is business. Ideally, its job is to make things or provide services, and employ people, while increasing the value of the company, either via a higher stock price or just turning a profit to stay in business. In an ideal world, those would not be mutually exclusive, and people would be treated fairly, acknowledging their labor with a living wage, and their lives with meaningful benefits. They shouldn't be treated as expendable, replaceable wage slaves. That kind of treatment has lead to strikes. And revolutions.

Government is in place for our common interests. At times government regulation can become oppressive and stifle innovation. But *laissez faire* capitalism can lead to corruption. Government is us coming together, and pooling our resources, to accomplish the things we deem are in the public interest, and for the public good. We elect representatives based on how we define those goals and how we think they should be accomplished. We pay taxes, and participate in the conversation of what is in our common interest. How that is defined can change over time, and based on which party is in power, but the idea remains constant. Taxes are not punitive. Obviously much of the disagreement over the years has been over who pays what share, along with how that money is used. But the "government is the enemy" argument has gained way too much traction in this country, and is often the misdirection used by corporations that simply don't want to pay more taxes, or be regulated. Their concern is profit, not mankind.

## AMERICA
## HAS A
## FREEDOM
## PROBLEM

We love our freedom. We're free to think, say, or write anything we want without fear that the Thought Police, or the actual police, will arrest us, then ship us off for some political re-education, and/or torture and/or death. And considering the misery humans have inflicted on each other over the millennia, it is something to treasure. The one most treasured aspect of living in America may be that no one fears the knock at the door.

We love celebrating the birth of our freedom and our divine origin story. Every Fourth of July we whip ourselves into a frenzy with flags, songs, hot dogs, and parades featuring marching bands, and girl scouts throwing shiny sticks in the air, followed by the grizzled old veteran in the wheelchair wearing the khaki-colored ice cream vendor hat, who contorts his mouth into a crooked, craggy smile as he slowly raises his arm to snap off a humble salute to the crowd. Then, as it hits golden hour, we turn our gaze to the sky as the jets fly overhead spewing out a smoky trail of red, white, and blue flatulence, and a tear falls from our eyes as we experience a gooey, simultaneous, patriotic orgasm.

I understand that people get choked up over symbolism but at times it can devolve into a kind of empty headed patriotism in which people fail to appreciate the subtleties of the ideas underneath it. Trying to grasp the yin/yang of individual desire and group responsibility seems to create a cognitive dissonance that sends most Americans running for a beer to make the thinking stop. Our popular notion of freedom is based on two big lies:

One: freedom equals license. Basically, I can do what I want, which is a child's understanding of the concept. Our political system is based on the rights of the individual in society, not the sanctification of the individual as some autonomous entity. Declaring everyone free is not the same as declaring life a free-for-all. It's something we experience individually and share collectively. And governments exist to safeguard it. Freedom is not selfishness. Imagine what traffic would be like if a segment of the driving public just decided they are free to go as fast as they want to get to their destination.

The moral lesson from being locked in our homes during Covid should have been that our lives affect each other. That we live in a society. A community. We thrive individually when we thrive collectively. We are in this together. Instead, many of us devolved back to a state of nature as we fought it out over toilet paper, the efficacy of masks, and the value of vaccinations.

The second assumption is that freedom equals laissez faire capitalism. That's why Republicans tend to criticize any law designed to regulate corporations as an "attack on freedom." But that's freedom perverted into a sanctification of greed.

AMERICA
HAS A
MONEY PROBLEM
AND A
HAPPINESS PROBLEM

Capitalism is, to paraphrase Churchill, the worst economic system, except for all the rest. At its best it celebrates individual achievement, hard work, and the benefits of having money, the most important aspect of which is not having to worry about money.

The upside of capitalism is that there is more human happiness in studying, working hard, taking chances, building something and reaping the rewards, whether it's money, personal satisfaction, a sense of accomplishment, or the feeling that one's life has meaning and purpose. It also creates a meritocracy, where one can rise into the upper class through hard work. In theory, anyone can buy a ticket. It's not about blood. It's about sweat. It's not a matter of being to the manor born. It's not a matter of birth, or breeding. Well, not completely.

There is more human fulfillment in personal accomplishment than in working your entire life in the service of the state. Communism may have arisen as a reaction against the abuses of capitalism, but it doesn't work when you attach actual people. You never end up with the dictatorship of the proletariat. Only the dictatorship of the dictatorship.

The downside of capitalism is that it's a celebration of wealth and conspicuous consumption, based on the theory that the value of a human life is equal to how much money one has and how many toys they can buy. We flaunt the attainment of wealth even more than we celebrate the inventions or contributions to society that lead to it. They used to be more closely connected.

Everything's either a hustle or a side-hustle. People are defined by being "millionaires" or "billionaires." Money has become the measure of a human life. It also changes the nature of work. Ideally, we work for ourselves and for each other. But that notion has been perverted into valuing wealth for its own sake, however it was achieved.

Get rich or die tryin'. Fake it 'til you make it. The advent of reality TV helped sell this concept. Giving fame to people with no discernable talent other than self-promotion. But this is no longer an aberration. It's the rule.

Years ago I railed against the fact that the Kardashians were famous for being famous and had no discernable skills or talent. What I didn't realize was that parlaying nothing into something was their talent. They have created a business model. In modern America, they've become the new paradigm. We've also traded investing for Crypto, and get high on the stories of fast money. Even the modern day Icarus that was Sam Bankman Freed hasn't sobered us up.

Instant money. Instant fame. Conspicuous consumption. The notion that wealth denotes morality and the right to power. All of these notions helped create the stage for the illusion that is Trump.

It also lead to a perversion of the idea of happiness. We're guaranteed life, liberty and the pursuit of happiness, but despite having a philosophical tradition founded in Socratic exploration for truth, we never stop long enough to define it.

We equate happiness solely with wealth and the pursuit of it. It's become the endgame of life instead of something that can enhance one's quality of life. There's the line: "I've been poor and I've been rich, and rich is better." I agree, it is. But we've equated the failure to succeed in business and accrue the benefits of wealth with a failure in life itself.

We're also greedy. People in many countries around the world are starving. There are places where "You can eat" is a lifesaving declaration. Only in America do we have "All You Can Eat." It's a celebration of gluttony. We're grotesquely obese because of our habits. We stuff ourselves with over-salted, high-calorie, over-sugared garbage, which decades of advertising told us is actual food, then react in disbelief at our expanding waistlines, and think it can all be solved by some miracle diet, juice cleanse, or magic shot. This not only lead to the proliferation of Type 2 Diabetes, but to the most insufferable, song and dance commercial on TV. And if anyone tries to tell us to change our lifestyle by not eating shitty food it's declared an assault on our freedom and government overreach. We're free to be you and me – only grossly overweight and unhealthy.

Falling through the cracks of a capitalist system can lead people to desperation. We all need food, shelter, and meaningful work. Or at least work. If people can't achieve the basics, they can land on the street. Or fall into depression.

Get rich quick schemes and instant gratification can lead to disappointment and happiness substitutes. Like drugs or alcohol. The reason drug cartels make billions is that they have millions of customers here in the U.S. An endless war on drugs has also resulted in the highest incarceration rate in the world. It's a vicious doom loop of chasing inflated goals, getting frustrated with failure, turning to substances to kill the pain, getting addicted, and spiraling out of control.

Trump realized a basic truth about Americans: we're malcontents. If we want it all, then by definition, we'll never have enough, and we'll always be looking at what someone else has, and getting pissed that we don't have it, while looking for someone else to blame.

Trump told his people that their anger is not only justified, but noble. They've also been told that what little they do have is being threatened by domestic liberal elites trying to change their way of life or by foreign invaders storming the border to sneak in and take it. All this makes us angry. And some people deal with that anger by taking it out on everyone else. And in America, we have the weapons of mass destruction to do it.

# AMERICA HAS A
# GUN PROBLEM

Crazy is a human problem. Armed and crazy is an American problem. Only in America do we provide the tools to inflict mass casualties when someone decides to pop off and take out their misery on the rest of us. That is social suicide.

There are 400 million guns in a country of 330 million people. There were over 40,000 gun deaths in 2023, including 22,000 suicides. There were 632 mass shootings. On average, over 300 people are shot every day, including children.

If those statistics were the result of air travel, we wouldn't be flying. If our food supply killed that many people, we'd plant our own gardens and have home testing kits for everything we eat. Yet we refuse to do anything about guns because we have an unholy fixation with them. And then there's the money. The gun industry is a $15 billion-a-year business and they will never give that up without a fight.

No civilized country needs this many guns. No other civilized country in the world has this many guns, or this many gun murders or suicides. We're not all hunters or sport shooters. We're gun nuts. We're armed to the teeth, and murdering each other at an unprecedented rate in a society that can breed economic desperation and mental illness.

But how did we get here? I grew up playing war in the neighborhood, using sticks as rifles, hiding in bushes, ambushing each other, making machine gun noises and screaming, "Bang! You're dead!" It was fun. When we were seven. Most of us grew out of it. Just not all of us. Like it says in 1 Corinthians: 13:11: *When I was a child I spake as a child, I understood as a child, I thought as a child. But when I became a man, I put away childish things.* Apparently we're not giving up childish things without a fight.

Perhaps it's rooted in our Revolutionary War origin story, threaded through our wild west gunslinger past, and then through our WWII mythology. We are victims of our romantic gun traditions. "The shot heard 'round the world..." "The rockets red glare. Bombs bursting in air..." Then we throw in a little Rambo to update the images.

Part of our mythology is the picture of the tough guy with a gun. The perfect paradigm for both the American myth and the American reality was actor John Wayne -- the strong, moral, movie tough guy, with his trademark swagger and take-no-prisoners attitude. His nickname was Duke.

Wayne was the star of classic westerns like *Stagecoach*, *Rio Bravo*, and *The Man Who Shot Liberty Valance*, along with WWII movies like *The Longest Day*. He became the living embodiment of the strong American male. Practically a meme before we had the concept of memes.

But it wasn't real. His real name wasn't even John Wayne. It was Marion Morrison. And he never served a day in the military. He was a college dropout who lost his scholarship due to an injury from body surfing and was rejected by the U.S. Naval Academy due to poor grades.

Still, he personified American swagger and the take-no-shit gun-toting hero. The good man who only drew his gun in self-defense, the perfect paradigm for the American military that, eventually, landed in Europe and kicked the shit out of the Nazis.

But the straight-up hero of the '40s, segued into the cultural confusion of the '60s. In the height of the mission creep clusterfuck that was Vietnam, when the country was tearing itself apart with protests and riots, John Wayne produced and starred in a war movie based on a song called *The Green Berets*, in which he tried to retrofit the black and white WWII myth of American right-thinking goodness into the fog of war that was Vietnam. The movie went so far as to strip a skeptical journalist character of his illusions, and eventually even adopt a young Vietnamese boy and re-name him "Johnny." It didn't matter that John Wayne was an illusion. He was a reality in the American mind.

Eventually the torch was passed to another actor -- Charlton Heston -- who waltzed onto a Colorado stage after

Columbine, at an NRA rally, defiantly held a musket in the air and uttered his stock, defiant mantra: "Out of my cold dead hands." I was not only shocked that he did this, but that he could shuffle on stage and raise the musket without knocking off his toupee.

Oddly enough, in Heston's case, this wasn't his political history. In the '50s and '60s he marched for civil rights, supported social programs, and was president of the Screen Actors Guild. He eventually went Republican during the Nixon years. Heston died in 2008. I'm not sure if anyone checked whether they pried the musket from his cold, dead hands, but either way, he set the tone for the defiant NRA reaction to mass murder.

It's also American culture. We celebrate violence. You can't go to a movie theater without seeing trailers for upcoming movies without guns in them. We just love shooting shit, whether it's cans off fence posts, woodland creatures in the forest, birds out of the sky, or each other.

Another pro-gun argument is that they're for protection. Bad guy with a gun, good guy with a gun. But it rarely works out that way. All those good guys with guns in Uvalde, who happened to be trained law enforcement officers, couldn't stop the one lunatic with an automatic weapon. Even if they stormed in immediately, the fact that he was already in there, shooting, rendered the argument false. Guns don't make us more safe. They make us more dead. In response to a Nashville school shooting, Tennessee lawmakers passed a bill that allows for arming teachers. Perfect. Why not just arm the students, wait for the low blood sugar tantrums to kick in, and see what happens.

On July 4th, 2020, there was a mass shooting at a parade in Highland, Park, Illinois. Former Education Secretary Bill Bennett, a conservative who spent years preaching about family values and personal responsibility, who was also a heavy gambler who blew millions in Vegas, opined that the killer needed an exorcism and that his actions were the result of spiritual problems. Matt Schlapp, head of CPAC, claimed

God was the answer. Schlapp has been accused of groping a male limo driver at a convention.

There's also the capitalism aspect and the fact that success in life is predicated on the money one makes. With the images of wealth and fame paraded in front of us in film, TV, music, and social media, it's no surprise that many people feel like failures, which breeds resentment, and anger. We're a very angry people. Economic pressure, poverty, homelessness, drugs, a political party sinking into a fascist abyss. Then add guns. What could go wrong?

Then there are the paramilitary types. 'Roided-out, jacked-up dudes with nothing to do with all the extra Testosterone. So they dress up in camo, flak jackets, and soldier hats, and do military cos-play. Or invade the Capitol.

Still, society needs to defend itself, and so, after every shooting, Democrats scream about enacting meaningful gun safety legislation. We had an automatic weapons ban in 1993 that lasted ten years until George Bush blew it away. After the 2017 Las Vegas mass shooting, when a maniac opened up on a crowd enjoying a country music concert, killing 58 people and wounding 500, government got its shit together and passed a law about "bump stocks," making it less easy to modify a certain rifle into a machine gun. That lasted until 2024 when the Supreme Court tossed it out.

Of course, we could always try to outlaw guns except those used for hunting. Or sell automatic weapons, but not the magazines, which would only be sold to gun ranges, clubs, and would have to be rented, like bowling shoes. People could own guns. Hang them on the wall. Admire them. Show their friends. But rent the bullets.

It could work. But it will never happen. The gun lobby is too powerful. The old west mentality is too ingrained in us. The constitutional "right" to own as many weapons as we want has been hard-wired into our national consciousness.

Despite all the Annie Oakley, Lauren Boeberts out there, it's mostly a guy thing. Guns are the imbecile's language. Bullets are the aggrieved loner's vocabulary. So much for standing on a streetcorner railing against the government coming for your stuff or taxes being too high. Words were once weapons. Votes were weapons. Now actual weapons are weapons. In maybe the most twisted part of all this is that we've normalized these shootings with terms like "death toll."

Meanwhile, the left screams about sensible gun reform while the right screams back about the Second Amendment, and politicians cough up the usual thoughts and prayers after a massacre, a pathetic cover for their fear of jeopardizing their jobs by taking a moral stand and incurring the wrath of the NRA.

Gun laws are necessary, but ultimately they're a Band-Aid on a sucking chest wound. Red flag laws. Buybacks. Universal background checks. Closing the gun show loophole. Mandatory waiting periods. Gun safes. Biometric triggers. Laws that punish parents if their child shoots someone with their weapon. While they will reduce the carnage, which is a good thing, it's also a relative thing. Guns in America are not going away. You'll have to pry them out of our cold, dead hands. Not even dead children will give them a come to Jesus moment. They love power too much.

For all the noble work of Fred Guttenberg, David Hogg and Moms Demand Action, it won't change the fact that we are nation of gun freaks hiding behind a flimsy legal justification, stoked by a dangerous mythology, playing out a toxic combination of old west mythology, economic anxiety, social isolation, and red state stupidity. If Americans need protection against being shot by other Americans then there's something fundamentally wrong with living in America. It's a miracle the country itself hasn't exploded. Maybe instead of asking why are there so many mass shootings in America, we should be wondering why there aren't more.

We've become comfortably numb to the never-ending violence. As Trump commented in early 2024 at a gathering in Iowa after another shooting which left a child dead: "Get over it." One might think he'd moderate his stance after nearly becoming another fatality, but the fact that he was at the GOP convention wearing a Maxi-pad taped to his ear made it clear that he would use the moment for all its martyrdom potential, and not as the basis for advocating gun safety laws.

# BECAUSE WE HAVE ALL THESE
# PROBLEMS WE HAVE A
# TRUMP PROBLEM

Trump is a Frankenstein monster of modern American culture. Religion as identity. Capitalism as a zero sum game. Reality TV. Fame for fame's sake. A celebration of greed and conspicuous consumption. The cheapening of honest work. Rewarding selfishness over service. A distortion of the concept of morality. Skepticism about education to the point of taking pride in ignorance. A suspicion of knowledge, and the death of truth. And a celebration of anger. We've not only legitimized his sins, we've lionized them. Trump has been reincarnated as the new American ideal.

He's the idiot's avatar. He spits in the eyes of the left and his people cheer. The dumber and more rapey he is, the more empowered they feel. Politicians have always pandered for the religious vote. Trump has weaponized it. And his personal behavior has nothing to do with it. Even his guilt on 34 counts of paying off a porn star to hide an affair during an election year while disguising the nature of the payments hasn't dissuaded his loyal followers. In fact, it's solidified their love for him. They get off on his defiance.

Roughly one-third of America is out of its fucking mind. Angry. Aggrieved. Ready to fight, kill, and die for a wannabe dictator. They draw their strength of purpose from Trump. Their identity. Their validity. Their morality. He is the chip on their shoulder, their defender against things they don't understand and things that scare them. Like education. Sexual fluidity. And science.

All these elements conspired into Trump's rise to the presidency, along with his treasonous attack on government to retain power. And his present attempt to retake it.

Some still hold to the notion that his support is rooted in economic frustration. They cite the famous Clinton war room adage of "it's the economy, stupid." It wasn't true in 2016. It's not true now. Those early hate rallies were filled with people chanting orchestrated 3-word slogans like "Build the Wall," "Drain the Swamp," and "Lock her Up!" And it was all because they were too poor or too stupid to travel to Hollywood and sit in a game-show audience chanting, "Wheel of Fortune!" I saw a lot of MAGA hats and shirts. I didn't see one sign that read, "I'm really upset that economic growth has stalled out at less than 2% of GDP!"

These people aren't economists any more than they're infectious disease specialists. And even if they have been getting hit by inflation, it's always been a fact of American life, to one extent or another. No one votes for a dictator because of the price of gas and eggs. Ok, maybe some do but they should just come out and admit that rising prices are really a smokescreen to hide the fact that they are frustrated by the complexities of modern American life and prefer the simplicity of dictatorship. Maybe they just want the trains to run on time.

They believe Trump's lies about the economy because they want to believe them. Putting on a MAGA hat demonstrates to the world that you're angry. And, dammit, you're going to take it out on someone. Trump knows his people. He knows how to rile up a crowd. He loves the poorly educated. And they love him back.

We just may be too dumb for democracy. Despite all his crimes, Trump still pulls crowds. Only Obama could pull those crowds. The difference was that the Obama crowds were calling for hope, while the Trump crowds were and still are calling for hangings. He's like the political version of an aging hair band, performing the hits without the original fire but it doesn't matter. MAGA's favorite activity is dressing up in red, going to a rally in the middle of a cornfield and singing in the rain under a downpour of liberal tears, while Trump lumbers on stage and dry humps the American flag.

Trump has a deep psychological need for power, and has happily inflicted his pain on an entire country, and the world, just to exorcise his own personal demons. Calling him an aspiring dictator isn't the conclusion. It's the premise. But the more dangerous part of it was how many were, and still are, eager to vote for him. Again, that's not on him; that's on us. The insecure, angry, racist, violent part of us for whom being American isn't an ideal, it's an identity. Even if the 14th Amendment couldn't keep him off the ballot, the American people should have banished him from the process. We didn't.

One might think that because we live in America that we'd grow better people. We don't. Some of that is based on the flaws in the system. Some is based on the flaws in being human. We're all vulnerable to the eternal human struggle. Jekyll vs. Hyde. God vs. the devil. It's been less than 100 years since Nazi Germany. That's a blip in human history. Human consciousness didn't evolve with the end of WWII. It just took us time to forget the horrors.

I've known for some time that the 2024 election would kick our insanity into overdrive. Just like during the Civil War, we are split along cultural, geographical, informational, and philosophical lines with little to no chance of healing. We are straining to hold on to ourselves. The forces of light and darkness are headed for a showdown in November. The problem is not as much what Trump did to this country as what he revealed about it.

In 2020, I published a book entitled *Death to America*. It came out right before the election. After Biden was elected, I thought about changing the title to: America's Near Death Experience, in that, for a brief moment, I felt we'd escaped the horrors of Trump by electing Joe Biden and returning to our senses. Even after the January 6th attack, and finally limping our way to the inauguration. There was momentary relief.

But something told me to wait. I had a sick feeling that it wasn't over. And it wasn't. Not by a long shot. We may have removed the tumor, but the cancer has spread.

We're heading into a world of chaos of our own making. This election could either save our democracy or bury it. And it's all centered around a Hitler fetishist and his cohorts of small men, petty tyrants, power-hungry maniacs, and deranged Christian fundamentalists. The 2024 election is shaping up to be a melee of a shitshow of a farce of a clusterfuck -- to quote the imbecile -- "Like the world has never seen!"

And the final act of this Grand Guignol is about to play out IRL.

# CHAPTER SEVEN

# THE 2024 ELECTION

# DEMOCALYPSE
# NOW!

America has gone mad. Mad as in angry. Mad as in crazy. The inmates aren't running the asylum, but they've got more than a few seats on the board. It's *Brave New World*, *1984*, and the zombie apocalypse all wrapped in the flag.

There have been times in our history – the Civil War, The McCarthy/Red Scare '50s, Vietnam, Watergate  -- where the country has been torn apart. Times where we have lost our way. Now it seems that we have lost our minds.

We're living in the Great Upside Down. Abnormal is the new normal. Hate is the new love. Dumb is the new smart. Believing is thinking. Stupidity is intelligence. Appearance is reality. Traitors are patriots. Criminals are victims. Selfishness is human nature. Schadenfreude is pleasure. Society is socialism. Fascism is patriotism. The Speaker of the House is a Jesus freak. State Supreme Courts are reviving 19th century anti-abortion laws and will be going after contraception if they get the power. House Republicans are raging like they've just done poppers on the dance floor. They'd already succeeded in convicting Hunter Biden, and were licking their lips at the prospect of impeaching Joe Biden, and indicting Dr. Fauci. Another sign of our full-tilt insanity -- a dedicated 80-year-old physician and public health professional with over a half century of public service needs full-time security to protect him from death threats.

Somehow American exceptionalism has devolved into American special needs, as our freedom-loving, 248-year-old democracy could be descending into a theocratic dictatorial oligarchy. Hanging in the balance is the definition of what it means to be American. Our well-being at home. Our power in the world. It's a sad, twisted irony that a country that came into being by overthrowing a monarch could end up being royally fucked.

What's so sick about this is that after everything Trump has done in this country, and to this country, he's still a thing. He's been convicted of election interference and sexual assault. He extorted a foreign ally to influence an American election. Colluded with an enemy to rig an election. Extorted a

Secretary of State to rig the state's vote count. Ran a crooked charity. Ran a phony university and paid $25 million to settle the resulting lawsuit. Cheated on his pregnant wife with a porn star and was convicted of paying her hush money disguised as legal fees to hide his activities during an election. He committed bank fraud. Tax fraud. Election fraud. He lied about a deadly disease. At this point, it's over one million deaths. They should put up a giant sign outside Mar-a-Lago keeping a running tally of deaths as if they were Big Macs. He attacked the government to overthrow an election. He threatened judges, their clerks, and their families. He sent a Christmas message telling his enemies to rot in hell. Yet, nothing seems to break the dictator spell.

Could fascism happen here? If so, it will take its own form. But Trump has brought us to the point that we're asking the question, and that, in itself, reveals the inherent danger.

Another weakness is our classic American assumption that no matter how bad things get, they will always work out for the best. That it's always darkest before the dawn. Instead of getting darkest before it gets really fucking bleak. The belief that goodness always prevails may end up being our Achilles Heel.

We've reached the third act in this movie, where it seems like the bad guys are about to win. They've routed the rebel forces, the emperor is gloating as he screws up his face and gives the order to finish them off. If it's *Star Wars*, this is the part where the rebel fighters, lead by our hero, appear out of hyperspace, storm the death star, and with one strategic shot, blow out their power source as the bad guys explode into space dust.

This is the happy ending culture we were raised in. It's embedded in our history, and our mythology. It's the myth that goodness always triumphs over evil. That the arc of the moral universe is long but it bends toward justice. That we're the good guys and we always do the right thing. We face adversity. We fight against evil. All seems lost, but then we win because God is on our side. Fucking Frank Capra and his

Hollywood endings.

Our popular fiction has lulled us into a false confidence and the illusion that our plucky, never-say-die American spirit will always prevail. We always thought our ideals were our greatest strength, but when it comes to Trump and his MAGA agenda, what we have is a failure of imagination.

Why is Trump running? It's his only play. He doesn't want the job. He needs the power of the presidency, along with the power of the military, to keep his ass out of prison, and take revenge on his enemies. His only move was to keep going forward and play it exactly as he's played every single accusation and lawsuit in his life: Denial. Defiance. Attack the accusers. Cry foul. Claim it's all rigged against him. Then try to rig it, himself. He riles up the base and tears at the fibers of our democracy like a hyena ripping the flesh off a dead zebra.

Trump never stops. He's still blasting out rabid, incoherent, Truth Social screeds while ensconced in his garish, gaudy, musty, rat and roach infested crack palace leisure dome country club with the pink sportjacket, leather-tanned crowd, staging New Year's Eve party spectacles featuring Vanilla Ice, a teenage mutant Ninja turtle and hordes of washed up, over-Botoxed geriatric prom queens sporting fake tits and fat lips, wearing couch upholstery dresses, blowsy blond wigs and gaudy jewelry.

The fat fuck also thinks he's going to live forever. He can't envision a world in which he doesn't rule, let alone one in which he doesn't exist. He is the world. It's an even more perverse pathology than Louis XIV's *L'Etat, c'est moi*. It's "I am the world."

When his opponent was President Biden, he attacked him at every turn, trying to stain his reputation by going after his son. Hunter Biden's laptop, Hunter Biden's taxes, Hunter Biden's dick. Hunter Biden's drugs. Hunter Biden's gun permit. They were the Benghazi, and Hillary's emails of the day.

He tossed around phrases like the "Biden Crime Family" because his favorite rhetorical trick is to accuse his enemies of exactly what he's doing. We all know he's corrupt. But he tries to brand everyone as corrupt to take the stink off of him.

They impeached Homeland Security Secretary Mayorkas to gin up the immigration issue, then sabotage a border bill of their own making, then screamed for an economic meltdown during an election year. They were working on a Biden impeachment until their star witness turned out to be a KGB plant. Then, in a demonstration of their allegiance to the dear leader, they show up at Trump's New York trial in matching Trump red ties, reciting pre-arranged talking points.

They try to subvert the voting process on every level, both federal and state. Voter suppression, attacking voting by mail, and trying to enable Republican state legislatures to override state courts when it comes to vote counting. And he's ramping up threats of violence at polling places.

They militarized every problem we've faced, both domestically and internationally. They know that whoever's in the White House bears political responsibility for the state of the world. Russia invades Ukraine? Biden's fault. Hamas attacks Israel? Biden's fault. Israel attacks Gaza. Biden's fault. Gas prices, inflation. Biden's fault. They could end up tracing the origins of the coronavirus to Hunter Biden's laptop. Will China invade Taiwan? Biden's fault. Everything's a political weapon. It doesn't matter if it's real or if these problems are infinitely more complex. It's not about the content. It's about the noise. They just want to throw hand grenades, watch the carnage and scream, "Biden's fault!" Now that Biden is out they will turn these same attacks against Kamala Harris.

These miscreants have power in our government. But they didn't elect themselves. They were elected by the voters in their districts, which is evident of the deeper intellectual and moral rot in this country. Instead of being public servants they are public performers. Their actions are a combination of political theater and performance art, centered on a single goal: power.

MTG, an androgynous three-toed spawn of a foot and a potato, with a girl crush on both original Jesus and Orange Jesus. She once cupped the balls of a Trump cutout at a rally. One wonders what she does to the Jesus statue in church when no one's looking. She probably would've given him a handy while he was on the cross, just to cement her name in the books.

Boebert gets felt up in a theater, crotch grabs her date and punches out her ex husband in a restaurant. I guess the take-away with Bobo is that if you spend time with her, go to the theater, not to dinner. She's up for re-election this year, and even switched districts to give herself a better shot.

Gaetz is a smarmy, greasy, heavily Botoxed nepo baby who was allegedly running underage girls for sex parties. Jordan is still dodging accusations from misdeeds as OSU. Gosar may be suffering from Parkinson's, which in many brings out their dignity but in him it's just the physical manifestation of his inner evil. Mike Lee. The cowardly traitor on January 6th on the phone with the White House crying, "Just tell me what to say!" Tommy Tuberville. Only in America could a state (Alabama) reject a class act like Doug Jones in favor of an ignorant big-eared dumbfuck football coach. And the only reason Doug Jones was ever elected was that he ran against an accused child molester. That's what it takes for a decent, intelligent person to win a red state senate seat.

Then there was George Santos. Essentially, dinner theater Trump. Santos was the living embodiment of our political decline. In the House, the mooks may have inherited the Earth, but they were just another "hold my beer" moment for Republicans in a Long Island district who elected an actual scammer to Congress.

Santos was not just a serial liar, but a *Catch Me If You Can* level con artist. But they voted for him. At least Trump's bio was accurate on the surface. Even if his company was run like a criminal enterprise, and his net worth and business acumen were a myth, at least he was reality-adjacent. Yes,

Santos was finally kicked out for being a political liability and replaced by a Democrat. But he was a living parody. Somewhere Andy Kaufman is kicking himself, pissed that he didn't think of running for office.

Mitch McConnell's batteries are running down and he's malfunctioning in public but will continue on in the great tradition of old school Dixiecrats of being wheeled onto the Senate floor nearly comatose yet able to cast a final vote by tapping a button, before drooling on his tie.

We have the best Supreme Court money can buy. Clarence the Big Red Judge, who called the Anita Hill hearings a high-tech lynching. I wonder if he considers being bought and paid for by a Nazi-loving billionaire high-tech slavery? Alito's wife hangs an upside-down American flag outside their home after January 6th to show her support for the attackers and it's business as usual. They will never recuse themselves from cases that have even the appearance of impropriety because that's not what power does.

Then there are the Trump trials. Even with the convictions he continues to weaponize his victimhood. He compares himself to Nelson Mandela or Alexei Navalny, a true martyr for a cause, declaring himself a "dissident." And his people cheer. He also understands the attention span of the American public is limited. We get bored easily. A former president could go on trial and the media covers it with Breaking News hysteria, but it could all get pushed off the headlines by a new iPhone release. He knows that time is always on his side. He is the living embodiment of six of the seven deadly sins: Pride, greed, wrath, envy, lust, and gluttony. Unfortunately, he's not guilty of the seventh sin of sloth – the very one you'd wish he'd succumb to.

Democrats have to respect this and fight accordingly. Trump will go down fighting. He beat the Mueller Report, two impeachments and thousands of lawsuits, very few of which he actually settled. He lost in 2020 but then tried to steal the election by claiming it was rigged against him. I'm convinced only reason he left D.C. was that military wouldn't back up his play.

Democrats couldn't stop him with the 14th Amendment but they were right to attack him with it. Attack him with everything. Just attack.

As I write this, the news flashed that Trump was found guilty on all counts in the Stormy Daniels Hush Money Election Interference case. The system occasionally works. Time will tell whether this has any political impact. Thanks to the Supreme Court, it will most likely be his only trial before the election. If he wins, and is allowed to take power, all the other cases go away. It won't matter if they're state or federal charges. That's what Democrats don't seem to get. If he's allowed back in power, he'll wipe them all away with a wave of his tiny hands, stand in the Oval Office and play come and get me.

Trump tried to use the 2022 midterms to set up accomplices in swing states to throw the 2024 election to him but ended up crapping out in Arizona, Michigan, Minnesota, Nevada, New Mexico, and Pennsylvania. Despite the pundits' predicting a red wave it didn't materialize. Other than J.D. Vance in Ohio, every deranged Trump candidate lost. Kari Lake, the Norma Desmond of Arizona; Dr. Oz, the crudité carpetbagger Oprah spawn in Pennsylvania; Doug Mastriano, the bullet-headed lox in Pennsylvania.

While he may not have succeeded in planting operatives in swing states, Republicans are still at work gerrymandering and screwing with election rules as best they can, like Governor DeWine in Ohio signing a bill to institute Voter ID; which is the reasonable-sounding rule that requires a picture ID to vote, but is specifically designed to disenfranchise Black people by making it more difficult to register. Trump's game plan is to do everything possible to steal the 2024 election, then cry foul if he loses.

In early June he was compiling his short list for VP, scanning the field of moral Jello molds to see who would be his literal partner in crime. Marco Rubio. "L'il Marco." It was always an appropriate nickname as Rubio not only looks small, he feels small. J.D. Vance, who seems to have painted on permanent eye makeup. Tim Scott. Byron Donalds, a Tim Scott wannabe. Ben Carson. Doug Burgum.

He had his pick of thirsty fembots, all hustling for his attention like it was some bizarre beauty pageant. Haley, Tulsi Gabbard, Nancy Mace. Kristi Noem, until she bragged about shooting a dog. I'm surprised he didn't stage a wet T-shirt contest. They're all so power hungry they'd probably do it. I assumed the second tier candidates, Elise Stefanik and Sarah Huckabee, would suffer from not being hot enough.

In the end, it was Vance who became Trump's mini-me and the son he never had. It didn't matter that Vance once said he never liked Trump, thought he was an idiot, called him noxious and reprehensible, and compared him to Hitler." In modern American politics, those are compliments.

## THE CHAOS FACTOR

As much as 2024 has been billed as a binary choice between two candidates, the election won't be. We tend to break elections down to the personalities involved, while ignoring the power of the times. Elections don't play out in a vacuum. Just look back at the last 65 years. There were always mitigating factors. There was always chaos.

In 1960 the first live TV debates favored telegenic JFK over sweaty Nixon. JFK won by a narrow margin, though some cast doubt on his rich father orchestrating some votes in Illinois. If it did happen, it's faded into history.

In 1964, LBJ ran against Barry Goldwater. It was during the civil rights movement, Vietnam, and the beginning of the counter culture revolution. It was our cultural metamorphosis, or our descent into indecency and moral relativism, depending on your point of view. We were beginning to face our racist and sexist demons. Goldwater was a staunch conservative, but was branded as a warmonger who was ready to drop atomic bombs on Vietnam. We'd already survived the Cuban Missile Crisis by hiding under our desks. No one was nuclear-curious.

LBJ's abdication, and the 1968 assassinations of MLK and RFK, as well as the shooting of George Wallace, set the stage for the violence in Chicago at the Democratic convention. There were riots in many cities and we saw the advent of the "law and order" campaign theme, with all its clandestine racist undertones. And no one knew that Nixon had arranged a backroom deal with South Vietnam to reject a peace proposal promising better terms if he was elected.

The war overshadowed 1972, as Democrats ran a good man in George McGovern, but it was the traditional wish-casting, as he had no chance of winning. As well, his campaign took a hit when it came out that his first Vice Presidential nominee, Thomas Eagleton, had been treated for mental illness. Nixon won easily. But then came Watergate, Nixon's resignation, and Gerald Ford's pardon.

In 1976 Carter was a cleansing breath of fresh air, after the stink of Watergate. But the chaos of inflation, high oil prices, gas lines, and the Iran hostage crisis were major contributing factors in 1980. Even with the Camp David accords that brokered a peace deal between Israel and Egypt, chaos came into play when Carter sent helicopters to Iran to rescue the hostages only to have them crash in the desert due to dust getting in the engines. Soldiers dead. Mission aborted. In theory, had he pulled off an Entebbe-style rescue he could have gone on TV and said "I believe in peace until the lives of Americans are threatened, then I act and act decisively." It may not have made all the difference but it might have given him a much-needed boost.

Ultimately, Carter was also no match for Reagan's telegenic personality, old-school flag waving, and his slogan: Make America Great Again. Americans were bored with Carter's introspection and yearned for some red, white, and blue smoke to be blown up their asses.

That lead to eight years of Reagan and trickle down economics. There was Iran/Contra. And there was AIDS, a major health crisis ignored by a president, who was suffering from the early stages of Alzheimer's. A fact that was not communicated to the public.

In 1988, George H.W. Bush beat back a weak Democratic challenger, who shot himself in the foot with an unfortunate photo-op of him riding on a tank. Boomers ushered in Bill Clinton in 1992. Again, young and telegenic beats old and out of touch. He was re-elected in 1996 against another old competitor and helped by a robust economy. But Republicans were not deterred. They spent five years investigating Clinton, with accusations ranging from a crooked Arkansas land deal to being responsible for his White House Counsel's suicide.

In 1998 they struck gold with the blowjob heard 'round the world, by which time *Fox News* was around to flog the lurid details. It lead to Clinton's impeachment, but not his conviction. But it still had legs in 2000, as Al Gore distanced himself from the scandal and hit the trail without Bill, while displaying whatever is the opposite of charisma, and was not able to electrify the electorate. It all came down to Florida, which was first called for Gore but then became too close to call, leading to the infamous recount, hanging chads, the Roger Stone-concocted Brooks Brothers riot, and the Supreme Court handing the election to Bush. But it was a third party candidate in Ralph Nader who siphoned Gore's votes in Florida, which handed the decision to the Court. That gave us Bush 41. And 9/11. The neo-cons. And two phony wars.

In 2004, Democrats picked John Kerry. They sold his experience as a Senator and his war record, having been shot three times. In contrast, Bush's war record also became a story in that he allegedly avoided Vietnam by fucking off in the Texas Air National Guard, which he allegedly got in thanks to daddy's connections. So, what does Karl Rove, dubbed Bush's Brain, do? He goes with his battle plan of attacking his enemy's strength instead of his weakness. He invents "swiftboating" getting a bunch of Kerry's Navy shipmates to challenge his service during the war and criticize his anti-war activities afterward. But Kerry never battled it back in kind. The lie gained a foothold in voters' minds by repeating it incessantly and by the media picking up on it and giving it airtime.

As a sidebar benefit *60 Minutes* also ran a story about Bush getting bounced out of the Texas Air National Guard, and when the validity of the sources was questioned, Dan Rather was bounced out of the network. It was win-win for Rove. Republicans also drove the fear of gay marriage playing the culture war games and that helped Bush win Ohio and the 2004 election.

Bush also threatened to privatize Social Security, saying in 2005: "I have some political capital and I intend to spend it." People were outraged. They descended on D.C. Bush backed off but the GOP wet dream of getting rid of what they pejoratively refer to as "entitlements" lives on.

That lead to 2008, the housing market crisis, a crashed

economy, and Sarah Palin. Which lead to Obama. Seemingly another cleansing moment, at least it felt like one at the time.

Despite Obama's shaky start in 2012, his Republican challenger, Mitt Romney, went down in flames, having stepped on his own dick with a private speech made public and his "47% remark." Democrats were able to brand him as an elitist with no connection to ordinary Americans.

But then in 2016, chaos reared its ugly head on several fronts. Our sexism and racism kicked in. Trump flogged the original Clinton scandal, jump-started by the Benghazi hearings, and attacked Hillary over a private email server. A third party candidate, along with a last-minute October surprise via the Comey letter, handed us Trump. In 2020, Biden's victory provided yet another cleansing breath but it was not the course correction it should have been. That lead up to the debate, Biden's withdrawal, and a new candidate, with less than four months to go before the election. And the chaos lives on.

This election has always been about the swing states. Just like in 2016 and 2020. As for the red states: fuck 'em. They're gone. In play are Arizona, Nevada, Georgia, Wisconsin, Michigan, Pennsylvania, and maybe North Carolina.

The traditional Democratic coalition could be hemorrhaging supporters, which could put swing states in jeopardy, particularly Michigan, with its Palestinian population. Young people might treat a vote for Republicans or Independents as a form of protest. Apathy or cynicism could result in some voters staying home. There's talk of Black and Hispanic voters peeling away.

Univision has been taken over and seems to have slanted right, which could hurt Democratic support among Hispanics. There's some machismo thing going on here that Democratic strategists need to get to the bottom of and somehow neutralize by shaming Trump and attacking his masculinity. Don't criticize him for being tough. Mock him for being weak. Destroy his image in the eyes of those who worship him. I think *pendejo* might be the appropriate slam.

Republicans know all they have to do is play to the political margins. Just cut down the number of Democratic voters on the A side through voter suppression and voter intimidation, like they tried in Philadelphia in 2016. Then screw with the count and/or certifying the results on the B side.

They lost midterm elections and Secretary of State positions in Arizona, Pennsylvania, Michigan, along with governorships, so they won't have allies in those states screwing with the results. Texas is trying to test state laws so that legislatures can override the voters' decision. There will be Russian involvement. There will be AI deep fakes. There will be mind-fucking. There will be threats of violence, if not actual violence. There will be lawsuits challenging state vote counts.

## THIRD PARTY CANDIDATES

Jill Stein and Putin gave us Trump. She pulled enough votes from Hillary Clinton in 2016 and she's ready to do it again. She isn't a green party environmentalist. She's a Russian asset. As is the gap-tooted phony from Princeton -- Cornel West. While the process absorbed and then spat out spiritual egomaniac Marianne Williamson, she was threatening to get back in the race, doing TV hits calling for an "open convention." Her arrogance and ambition border on smarmy. RFK is still around, brain worm and shady past notwithstanding. If he didn't have a famous father he'd be selling vitamin supplements out of a van. Allegedly a drunk who drove his ex-wife to suicide, he's an anti-vaxxer with delusions of grandeur. That doesn't mean he won't be a factor if his candidacy gives disaffected Democrats a place to go. No Labels crapped out but it's still early. They could return in some other form.

Either Russians and/or Republican PAC money, or both, are behind Stein and West. What his game plan is – who knows? With his ridiculous Man in Black costume, the psycho hair and the phony preacher patois. He supposedly owes thousands in back alimony. But he's not stupid. He knew the effect running third party could have on Black Democratic support, though that was before Kamala Harris became the nominee. Who knows if it was for the Rubles or the megalomania. Something turned him from social justice warrior to election terrorist. Or maybe he just had the desire to go down in history alongside Ross Perot, Ralph Nader and Jill Stein.

## THE BORDER.

In 2015 Trump threatened to deport 11 million people, which journalist Jorge Ramos tried to call him out over and got thrown out of a press conference by Trump's long-time bodyguard. And those were the good old days. After throwing kids in cages and separating families, he's come back around to calling for the same mass deportations and deploying local vigilantes to deport anyone who looks illegal. Yeah, that'll work out fine.

Trump is just playing the hits. He'll probably cycle back around to "build the wall." Even though he claimed he'd already built it, which he didn't, it won't matter. The crowds will chant and cheer because that's what they've been trained to do. He even coined a new phrase: "Migrant Crime," which he's testing out at his rallies.

Republicans will continue to stage photo ops at the border. It's one of their favorite party tricks. Tim Scott and Lyndsey Graham went down to take a few selfies. I wonder if they stole off to a villa in Cabo when the press turned their backs.

Republicans will scream about immigration and crime. They're not problems to be solved. They're weapons. They will make more inroads into the Latino vote screaming about "socialism," evoking memories of the corrupt governments many risked their lives to escape.

## ABORTION

Trump killed Roe v Wade, with an assist from Mitch McConnell. This should fire up women, as it did during the late 2023 elections in Virginia, Kentucky, and Ohio. The IVF Alabama Supreme Court decision should also fire up Democrats. Trump knows he'll be hit with this but he's already trying to tack to the middle to grab suburban women. He takes credit or avoids blame, depending on the occasion and the audience.

In September 2023, he tried to skate to the left, proclaiming that there's a compromise on abortion or that he's fine with letting it be decided by the states, claiming that's what most people want. It was complete bullshit but it wasn't challenged in the moment. Just as it wasn't fact-checked in the debate.

Democrats will most certainly point out that in 2016, when Chris Matthews asked if there should be some punishment for abortion, Trump hesitated, thinking what would play politically, then stated that "yes, there must be some form of punishment." But it won't matter. Unless they successfully brand him with it, he'll continue to say what he needs to say, like he's "evolved" since then. For a party that stubbornly refuses to accept evolution, the art of evolving on an issue is their escape hatch from any claims of hypocrisy.

For a fat fuck Trump is incredibly nimble at surfing the opinion wave. He knows all that's important is to ride it out. Whatever's playing around election day will be what he's for. After the election, it's a brave new world. He'll happily put kids in cages, embryos on pedestals, women and doctors in prison, and he'll instantly sign a federal abortion ban.

## THE ECONOMY

For a phenomenon that seems to be all about numbers, the economy is actually more about feelings. Biden resurrected the country from the Trump economic crash.

Unemployment is way down. The stock market is way up. We're no longer talking about recession. The Fed may cut interest rates before the election. Gas prices are high but coming down. There are shovel-ready projects ready to go. Factories are being built to bring manufacturing back home. Many in the media declared that people weren't feeling it but that's because Democrats haven't sold it. They've missed the chance to frame the narrative. You can't just repeat the phrase "infrastructure bill" without doing the appropriate photo ops in swing states and selling the idea that after Trump locked people in their homes, Biden put America back to work.

## THE WORLD

The Middle East has always been a powder keg but after the monstrous attack on October 7, and Israel's brutal retaliation, and the ongoing conflict, it's worse than not being able to thread the needle. It's that you can't even find the needle. There's no room for a clear moral stance. Support the Palestinians you're anti-Semitic. Support Israel, you're pro-genocide, or the appearance of it. None of the typical language will suffice. The pictures are horrifying and powerful. Trying to parse the difference between being anti-Semitic and anti-Zionist or pro human rights are distinctions meant for a college classroom but are way over the heads of most people. They react emotionally to the images, as anyone would.

We have to support our traditional ally in the region without condoning the deaths of over 20,000 Palestinians, amid starvation and accusations of genocide. Failing to condemn this may also lose some of the youth vote. A major political move, let alone a humanitarian one, would be to work out a peace deal based on a two-state solution with the cooperation of all the Arab states and the U.N. Though it is in the works, its success seems doubtful, given the history and the forces on all sides.

One might think that after 75 years of carnage greater minds would come together to find solutions to the problem.

But it will always be sexier to wave a flag, chant a slogan, and murder one's opponents in the name of goodness than to sit down at a table and hammer out a deal. Even if 99% of Israelis and Palestinians wanted to live together in peace, the remaining 1% will make sure to blow something up just to get the anger flowing and subvert it. There's also the war in Ukraine, which Putin knows he just has to wait out. It's the same play as McConnell in 2016 with Garland's nomination. Make your move and bide your time.

Wars are also raging in Yemen, and Syria, and refugees flee to safety in stable European countries, but it has tripped local backlash. Drug gangs run rampant all over Mexico, Central and South America, and Africa, all using weapons manufactured by the major world powers.

And we're not the only country in the world flirting with dictatorship. Sweden has a right wing government. As does Italy. There's a growing right wing movement in Germany, despite how that worked out the first two times. Many countries, including Italy, Poland, Austria, Belgium, and the Netherlands have populist movements that are gaining support, as reflected in the June, 2024, European Parliamentary elections.

Macron called for a new election. Marine Le Pen has been knocking at the fascist door for years and it momentarily appeared that the French were going to let her in, but then her party only pulled off a weak, third place showing. But each time they run they seem to get closer. And somehow, amidst this chaos, England booted out the Tories and voted the Labour Party back in.

There are totalitarian regimes in Russia, China, North Korea, Cuba, Poland, Hungary, Argentina, Turkey, and The Philippines. In late 2023, Argentina elected another lumbering Trump impersonator in Bolsonaro, then kicked him out. He tried to coup his way back in but was recently arrested. In Venezuela, Maduro seems to have lost an election, bigly, but in true dictator fashion, declared himself the victor. Whether this is in the zeitgeist, or human beings falling prey to their worst instincts, life on Earth seems to be devolving.

Maybe we just need to unplug the world and plug it back in. Or re-boot it in safe mode.

### THE DEMOCRATIC CANDIDATE

To paraphrase the great Donald Rumsfeld, "You go into an election with the candidate you have, not the one you wish you had." Up until recently, Democratic hopes had been resting on the shoulders of Joe Biden.

Biden has always been better at doing the job than getting the job. He tried in 1988. 2008. Backed off in 2016. But 2020 was his time. He was the moral alternative to the chaos candidate. But in 2024, he was the guy in charge with two wars raging, and an economy he should have been able to sell as in great shape considering where we were four years ago. But it just wasn't playing. That was because the administration didn't sell it from the beginning. And Biden wasn't skilled at communicating it.

His decency and experience may have been the antidote for four years of Trump mania, setting the stage for a post-Watergate, Carter-like return to decency, but we have short memories, along with inflation, high gas prices, and a dumb electorate. Democrats still fall back on a penchant for throwing statistics and policy at voters instead of framing the larger themes.

Biden was never a rhetorical fireball. He doesn't do oration. He walks on stage with a hesitant, old man shuffle, hands swinging by his side like salamis hanging in the window of a New York deli. He speaks in old guy speak, crooking his finger to make a point, sometimes getting sidetracked by the occasional gaffe or rambling story.

His speeches were monotonous, in the truest sense of the word. There were no dramatic pauses. He raced through talking points, so that they all blended into a single high-pitched whirr, like turbines on a factory floor. He often left out the definite articles making them feel even more rushed, and frantic.

He is, at heart, a good man, an experienced, dedicated public servant, and a savvy politician. He is sincere. And honest. But the age question was in the air as we headed toward that first debate. And then – disaster.

It was apparent the moment Biden walked on stage with the old man shuffle. They didn't even coach him on how to walk. And that was before he uttered a single word. Then he did, and shit went from bad to worse. The stakes were high, but no one anticipated a full-on meltdown.

Fuck the excuses. He had a cold. It was late. He'd been travelling. He looked pale. Doddering. Lost. If you're explaining, you're losing. Forget that Trump was firehosing lies from start to finish. The mistakes were agreeing to the debate in the first place, as well as no fact-checking which is like removing doping rules on horses before the Kentucky Derby. Trump just adjusts his shit to the rules. If there's fact-checking he sticks closer to the traditional bullshit. If not, he's off to the races.

And the clean-up didn't work. Rallies, public appearances, and a one-on-one interview with George Stephanopoulos didn't calm down the furor. Frankly, that sit-down had all the journalistic objectivity of an episode of To Catch a Predator.

Weeks later, people on both sides of the argument were freaking out. Democrats were firing missiles at each other. The circular firing squad was locked and loaded with calls for him to withdraw getting louder and more frequent. And from every camp. Even his staunchest political allies urged him to drop out, fearing down-ballot repercussions, while others offered tepid, cleverly worded public support. I can only imagine the conversations that were going on in private based on internal polling. Of course, in true fashion, the media flogged the shit out of it. They were in their sweet spot of a legitimate story and "breaking news" hysteria.

At this point, it's academic. If he wanted to regain his footing he would have had to recalibrate the way he carried himself. If he wanted to come off as powerful he didn't need to speed up and get more hyper. He needed to slow down. Take stage. Breathe. Just speak from the heart. Communicate not only his experience and understanding of the issues but his compassion and awareness of the struggles of average Americans. And an awareness of his situation along with the danger of Donald Trump. Stock phrases like "Don't compare me to the Almighty, compare me to the alternative" may have hit home at some point, but they came off as rote.

He needed to create moments. Let the thoughts ring out. And stop yelling. Raising your voice is not a way of communicating the importance of what you're saying. It makes you seem more out of control. And desperate.

He needed to avoid the cliché old-man finger pointing and pointless phrases like "I'm not kidding around," or "this is no joke." He was the Democrats' version of George H. W. Bush. Experienced, but possibly no match for Bill Clinton's charm and rhetorical style. Just as Jimmy Carter was no match for Reagan's actor skills.

And if this wasn't enough chaos, we had the shooting in Pennsylvania. Four months from the election and we'd already hit attempted assassination.

The question with Biden was never whether he could govern. It was whether he could win, considering the growing concern about his age. It became the elephant in the room. And the fact that experienced Democrats called for him to pull out revealed internal polling that must have been a disaster. Their public statements revealed their private knowledge. Then Biden got Covid. Which seemed to be the final blow. Now he's out. Harris is in. And it's a new ballgame.

# I HATE TRUMP

In case it hasn't been clear, I hate this motherfucker. I have screamed about him to anyone who would listen since he started his birther bullshit against President Obama in 2011 and then rolled down the escalator in 2015 with the blow-up doll wife and the actors he paid fifty bucks apiece to stand on top and cheer. And no, it's not Trump Derangement Syndrome, any more than a firefighter has fire derangement syndrome.

This is the fourth book I've written on the Trump phenomenon, along with writing numerous articles and doing radio/podcast hits, and I am completely fucking sick of him.

I'm sick of the way he's dominated our politics and our lives. I'm sick of screaming at my TV every night. I'm sick of writing his name. Sick of looking at his imbecilic face with the orange/bronze goop on it and listening to the firehose of horseshit that spews from his anal cavity of a mouth. I'm sick of that ridiculous cotton candy confection on his head. The dumpy suits and the dick compensator ties. The moronic, two-fisted bouncy dance. I'm sick of his Truth Social screeds. Sick of hearing his name every night on the news. I'm sick of the fifteen-word vocabulary. The incessant nonsensical bragging. The insane, rambling speeches about windmills and sharks, and boat magnets, and tributes to the late, great, fictional Hannibal Lecter. Not word salad as much as word salad with brown, soggy, wilted lettuce and bugs crawling all over it then thrown in the dumpster in a back alley on a hot summer day salad.

I'm sick of spending every day waiting for him and his crime family to be thrown in prison – the place he's belonged all his life. I'm sick of waiting for this country to shit him out of the body politic like the turd he is, wipe away the stain, and move on to fulfill our promise.

I hate that the news still hasn't completely figured out how to deal with him. Every story. Every headline. Every podcast. Every article. Every X/Twitter post. The world revolves around him. He must be in megalomaniac, egomaniac, narcissist heaven. I'm reminded of the Oscar Wilde line: "The only thing worse than being talked about is not being talked about" and damn if he hasn't gotten that in spades. He's even showing major signs of brain damage. He rambles, incoherently. Freezes when his Teleprompter malfunctions. His dentures slip when he tries to say "United States" and it sounds like he's gargling a mouthful of shit. In a pre-recorded video he started salivating. He shoots Adderall snot rockets out of his nose. This is where we are. A presidential candidate literally foamed at the mouth during a video, and the campaign released it. And he's still in the running.

Trump has dominated our lives for close to fifteen years! In politics. Out of politics. Winning. Losing. Being sued. Indicted. Convicted. Ranting on X/Twitter and Truth Social. Having his first wife "fall down a flight of stairs" or what Putin refers to as "dying of natural causes," then burying her on his golf course.

Trump is a moron. If he's talking he's lying. He confuses the simple-minded, while playing to their worst instincts. He ennobles the ignoble, empowers the powerless, and legitimizes the illegitimate. He is our ugliness personified.

And the grift never ends. His ho-bag daughter-in-law is on X/Twitter, shilling for donations. Trump sells NFTs, and you can buy 47 of them for around $4600, plus if you act now you get a piece of fabric from the suit Trump was wearing when he got indicted. Because of course they cut up the actual suit.

(For anyone who's interested I'm selling scraps from the Shroud of Turin on eBay, with a Certificate of Authenticity signed by Jesus himself. Just $19.95. Along with a money-back guarantee if you're not satisfied. And if you act now you can get two Turin scraps for the price of one. BOGO. Just pay an extra fee. Which is not getting one free because there's an extra fee.)

Then he follows it up with selling gold-leaf sneakers for

$400 and saying the Blacks will like him because they like sneakers and can relate to being stuck in the legal system. Then he hawks a leather Bible for $60.

He's a humanoid cartoon. A sociopath. A megalomaniac. He's not just egotistic. He's egoistic. He's not just the nucleus in an atomic particle. He's the totality. The singularity.

The final solution for Donald Trump? I propose a mandatory retroactive abortion. Dig up his mother then stuff Trump inside a cannon and shoot him back up into her uterus with such force that he explodes back into his component parts, as his daddy's sperm shoots out of her mouth and his mother's egg flies out of her asshole, and he just vaporizes. Disappears. Never to be born again.

I guess everyone needs a little wish-casting every now and then.

# TRUMP IS THE DANGER
# BUT THE PROBLEM
# IS US

This raging shithead pussy grabbed his way into the White House. And he could possibly do it again. But all he's ever done is make his play. The American people put him in office. No matter what the Russians did. No matter how he screamed "rigged" before 2016 and during and after 2020. In a decent, moral, intelligent country he would never have gotten a single vote. That's not on him. That's on us. Our American gremlins have been released. But it's our fault for feeding them after midnight.

It's not just the harm he's brought to this country but what he's revealed about it. We're not the people we thought we were. We're not the people we were told we were. Or to be more specific, a deranged part of us has figured out how to elect their own kind to public office, as well as getting three of them on the Supreme Court, while manipulating the levers of power to force their dystopian Angry God vision of America on the rest of us.

On paper, we are the shining city on the hill. But that's never been our reality. We've had our shining moments but they've been eclipsed more recently by dangerous fascist trends.

Because we assume that democracy is a debating society, we are consumed by the narcissism of small differences. Instead of seeing the common threat and uniting to defeat it, we are drowning in the quicksand of the culture wars. And "wokeness" whatever the hell that really is. Its original meaning, which described someone who was culturally aware, has been weaponized to imply a militant social justice warrior insisting on verbal and behavioral purity in every aspect of life. Like something out of the Chinese communist cultural revolution. I don't know if this is actually a movement or the extremes of a movement being used to negate the whole.

We are in danger of drowning in a sea of small differences, which could carve away at the political margins and enable a dictator to slip through. The 2024 election will be a battle not just for the heart, mind, and soul of the country but for the definition of the country. Whether we are a democracy and a pluralistic society or a Christo-fascist theocracy.

Over 2000 years after Christ and we're still locked in a struggle between good vs. evil. And one political party, in collusion with a media empire, is doubling down on evil. And Democrats continue to moralize, failing to remember that you cannot reason evil out of existence or shame it away. You need to destroy it. A struggle we naively thought we'd left behind in the 20th century.

If America falls, what hope is there for the rest of the world, not just in terms of decency, but military superiority? Without American support, less powerful democracies might not have the ability to defend themselves against Russian aggression, Chinese economic influence or North Korean madness. Trump was ready to sell out NATO in 2016. That will be first on his hit list in 2025. Retreating into isolationism has never been effective. It's always been a false choice. The 20th century world was co-dependent. The 21st century world is literally interconnected.

I made the mistake of focusing on Trump as the cause instead of the symptom of an American disease. It's not that we went dark. It's that our dormant darkness has reared its ugly head.

We found the worst person in the country, and gave him the most important job on the planet. And we could potentially do it again. This is our American psychosis. Our schizophrenia. Our deep stupidity, insecurity, anger, and racism. Being American doesn't automatically render us better people. And contrary to the American myth, the good guys don't always win. We've always had a talent for fighting foreign dictators but it's hard to believe we've got to fight a home-grown domestic one.

It's meaningless to say he is or isn't Hitler. He's our American Hitler. He's working from that playbook. His current rap about vermin and getting ride of communists, socialists, and fascists is straight from the Nazi canon.

It is a sign of our dysfunction that at this point we are even entertaining this conversation. We allowed Joe McCarthy in, and then eventually expelled him. But, unfortunately, we're at the point where "At long last, sir, have you no sense of decency" won't work. There will be no Republican senators telling Trump they don't have his back like they did with Nixon. They had their chance to convict him in two impeachment trials in the Senate and could have banished him politically. They didn't. They wouldn't cut him loose then. And they won't now. There is no crime or sin he could commit or be convicted of that would tear them from his breast.

He's still holding his rallies and the toothless hordes are still turning out, flaunting their MAGA hats, waving their flags, and dancing their fat asses off. And the Blacks For Trump guy is still in the background. Who says Trump hasn't delivered Black jobs.

In our mythology we respect people who have fought against tyranny and injustice, even putting their lives on the line. Washington, Adams, Jefferson, Lincoln, Gandhi, MLK, Mandela, Vaclav Havel. Lech Walesa. The guy who stood down a Chinese tank during the uprising in Tienamen Square. The people on the street during the Arab spring. Boris Nemtsov. Alexei Navalny. Vladimir Kara-Murza. The women of Pussy Riot, While we idolize them I don't know if we're ready to put ourselves on the line in the same way.

Or are we just paying lip service to that admiration. Are they really our heroes or do we have more of a forbidden love for those wild west antiheroes. People who defied the odds and ventured outside accepted norms, or outside the law.

Is humankind hell-bent on suicide? Is that the direction we're going? Is this a fork in the road or just a minor detour. A blip on an EKG or an indication of some deeper more basic human problem? Or is it just the ebb and flow of human behavior. What happens when our demons gain too much power? In the eternal human struggle, 248 years is just a blip in time. The great democracies of the past left a philosophical record of their ideas for others to build on but yet the governments and societies they virtually created also crumbled.

I'm curious how history will look back at this time. Assuming there still is history, as it's always the winners who get to write it. Will the American people sober up before November, 2024? Will they finally realize the danger in this moment? It's doubtful. If the American people had any real sense of who we are, and where we are, we wouldn't be here.

We are not a wise people. I'm reminded of a line from *Lawrence of Arabia,* in which Peter O'Toole's title character speaks to Omar Sharif, saying: "As long as the Arabs fight tribe against tribe, so long will they be a little people, a silly people. Greedy, barbarous, and cruel." The same could be said for us.

## IF TRUMP LOSES WILL TRUMPISM REMAIN?

What if he loses? He'll never concede or admit that he lost but that won't matter. Let him scream all he wants. He can't scream himself back into power. But what about MAGA?

My first instinct is that if you cut the head off the snake it will break the spell and his hold on people. There is no one else that could capture them like he has. On the other hand — there was Jesus. They killed him but his followers still managed to cobble together a movement that has sustained in its various holy and unholy forms for over 2000 years.

American democracy is only as valid as the hands in which it's been placed at any given time. Even if Trump quits, bugs out of the country, is beaten in the election, we still have to cure the Trumpism inside us. A Pandora's Box has been opened and the evils are flying around.

The MAGATs may never surrender the idea of Trump. He represents the notion that any slob can live in a gilded palace along with a mail-order Barbie doll wife. He is their hope. Their savior. Their redemption. These people are all in on theocracy, oligarchy, and some form of dictatorship. They've been empowered and they're not giving it up without a fight. Whether his followers can be seduced into lining up behind a new golden calf remains to be seen. It's always possible. His imitators will try to carry the mantle forward like fat, latter-day Elvis impersonators.

There's Dollar Store Trump, Ron DeSantis, who bullied his way to Iowa then jumped on the Trump express. A smarmy, venal, Napoleonic little martinet with his Imedla Marcos/Jackie Kennedy wife, right down to the long, flowing dresses and the elbow-length white gloves. He's the modern mash-up of Augustus Gloop and Benito Mussolini, with a little Juan Peron and the Shah of Iran thrown in. The power couple tried to morph into the absolute power couple. Fighting Disney, the state's largest employer. Fighting the culture wars with Don't Say Gay bills, while prancing around disaster sites in his My Little Pony boots. He threatened to start slashing throats the moment he got to Washington. Even on the level of the usual Republican tough guy rhetoric, most candidates don't go borderline homicidal.

Nikki Haley tried to pull an inside straight by not pissing off the MAGA base but only lightly criticizing her former boss. She managed to issue statements, make speeches and do TV hits making sounds like she was saying something, while trotting out every candidate platitude, and dancing around making an actual point like she was dodging raindrops. Railing against Biden, socialism, whatever tropes were lying around, she placed third in Iowa and still gave a lame victory speech. She lost New Hampshire and even her home state of South Carolina. She was even afraid to declare that the Civil War was about slavery or comment on Trump's rape trials. She should have been offended by Trump on several levels: as a woman, and as the child of immigrants.

She's still sniffing around the presidency, biding her time, trying to thread the needle by not insulting Trump or criticizing anything he's said or done. She'll continue to float out her origin story, proud of her Indian heritage, though not quite so proud as to hang on to her actual name. She obviously took the job with Trump as Ambassador to the U.N. to pad her resume, especially within the party, and raise her profile.

Trump tagged her "birdbrain," though "Slick Nikki" might have been closer. Despite the insults, and refusing to endorse Trump, she flip-flopped back to announcing her support. And, pre-convention, she released her delegates. She would have happily taken the VP nod, then played for time. Or the actuarial tables.

Tim Scott showed up at Trump rallies putting on a 21st century minstrel show to the point that he might as well have put on burnt cork and tap shoes and practiced his plantation speak. That was after crapping out with his own presidential run, which involved the magic act of making a fiancé appear out of nowhere to quell the gay rumors. Her name was Mindy. It might as well have been Mary, as in Hail Mary. He was so arrogant that he posted sunset beach pictures of him on one knee proposing to her. It was just a still photograph, no audio, so no one knew what he was actually proposing.

Vivek Ramaswamy, the bizarro world Obama. He mistakes Trump's allure with his voters for just being a snarky asshole.

Republicans have already tipped their ultimate game plan with the Heritage Foundation's Project 2025. They're coming for the New Deal, and will work their way through LBJ's Great Society -- Social Security and Medicare -- along with the Civil Rights Act and the Voting Rights Act. Then they'll eventually get around to Obamacare, which is Trump's white whale. They'll knock out a federal abortion ban, then go after gay marriage, and contraception. They have the single-minded desire to win, and the willingness to cheat. They have the guns, and the urge to do violence if they lose. And they have the misplaced certainty that God is on their side. They claim this is their second American revolution, which will be bloodless, "if the left allows it."

Even if it's not half the country but a vocal incensed minority they have found a back door to power.  We're only as strong as our weakest link, and that can create an opening for those with bad intent to use the system to game the system, and eventually destroy the system.

Trump may be the singularity into which American Democracy disappears. The black hole that sucks in all the decency, and rationality in the country. MAGA may be proof that a decent majority is no match for an angry, ill-informed, dis-informed, uneducated, angry, violent minority. A dumbed-down society is a dumbed-down electorate.

Sometimes it feels like we're less of a country and something more akin to the old joke about the unhappily married couple in their 80s who are putting off getting a divorce because they're waiting for the kids to die.

Honestly, I just can't see the way forward. I imagine there is one, but I just can't see it. The other day I saw a guy in a local burger place, wearing a MAGA hat and a smart-ass,

XXXXL anti-Democrat t-shirt. He was about 350 pounds, and the first thought that came to mind was that I bet those shirts didn't come in small or medium. And he was not being subtle. He was loud, proud, and defiant. The look on his face said he was not ready to engage in an honest, spirited dialogue about the issues facing us. These people have been given a taste of power and they're not giving it up without a fight.

I have heard from many not to disparage the MAGATs, and that there is no future in giving up on communication. Engage your drunken Trump uncle at Thanksgiving. See if you can find common ground. No. This is pointless, and emblematic of Democratic weakness. There is a middle ground for discussion when the subject is marginal tax rates, foreign policy, government spending, corporate regulation, energy, both fossil fuels and alternative. Not just the realities of those topics but the way they are handled. But when you are fighting an enemy that never quits and will do anything to win in a zero sum game that is not the time to play hands across the water. People say don't insult them, they'll just get mad. What more can they do? Support a dictator? They do. Attack the capitol? They did.

It's time to attack. We already start with one hand behind our backs because we tend to fall back on reason, and not violence. And these people are beyond reason. We need to speak the same language and live in the same reality before we can hit conversation and communication. You can't talk someone out of a cult. They must be defeated. Then deprogrammed. This isn't a rom-com where the initial sparks lead to passion. It's D-Day.

## COULD THIS BE BIDEN'S
## KOBAYASHI MARU?

After everything Trump has done, he shouldn't even be a thing. He should never have been a thing, but especially now. If cancellation were actually the thing the right claims it is, how is it that he hasn't been cancelled? Something's not playing. Trump scowls in a New York city courtroom, bitches on Truth Social, and shrieks to cameras on the courthouse steps while Biden flies to the Middle East trying to solve a major crisis, and yet it didn't play. It didn't move the needle.

And now, since Biden will be in office through the election and up until inauguration day: If Trump wins, either via the electoral college, cheating, third-party vote siphoning, or by any other means, what will he do about it? Will he surrender our Democracy even if it means losing it? That's exactly how Hitler became Chancellor of Germany. And the rest was history, or nearly the end of history. As noted by Goebbels, the weakness of democracy is that it provides its enemies with the means by which it is destroyed.

Will he allow a peaceful transfer of power to a dictator? Do you adhere to the rule of law if it means sacrificing the rule of law? He could concede and leave office, which would be like going out on a date and leaving the kids with the molester babysitter. What would his options be? His final act in an over 50-year life in politics could determine the course of history. This could leave the president with a seemingly unsolvable problem, one that fans of *Star Trek* might recall as the Kobayashi Maru.

In the 1982 film *Star Trek 2: The Wrath of Kahn*, Captain Kirk talked of a challenge from his cadet days. His method for solving an unsolvable problem was to rig the test. Spock calls it back later when he faced a similar no-win situation and sacrificed himself for the ship and the crew saying, "The needs of the many outweigh the needs of the few... Or the one." He then asks Kirk what he thought of his solution. Then he dies. I still choke up thinking about it.

So, if you could go back in time and prevent Hitler from taking power within the system would you do whatever it took to stop him?  In that scenario, Biden could have three choices.

## ONE
## MAKE TRUMP AN OFFER
## HE CAN'T REFUSE

One difference between 2024 and 2020 is that the president has control of the military and intelligence services. There is no Deep State but let's just say, for discussion purposes, that there is. Use the power you have while you still have it.

Send Trump a message before the election. Given his convictions for federal crimes, and the fact that he could eventually face more trials, convictions, financial ruin, and possibly prison, give him a way out: Make some excuse to pull out of the election. Then pack your shit and take off. Get on the plane and go to some country that doesn't have an extradition treaty with the U.S. Like Russia. Or stay and take your chances in the election, and an uncertain future. Prison is an ugly place. Anything can happen. Just ask Jeffrey Epstein.

His reaction might be surprising. Game respects game. It would be a play that no one would see coming because no one would see it, and frankly no one would believe it, even if it came out.

I imagine that Trump's already got a go-bag at the ready in case he loses and can't assemble his monkey army to protect him. And even if he did send the chimps to fight for him, they would be easily defeated because he doesn't have control of the military.

Give Trump a taste of his own tactics. Play hardball while you own a hardball. He might even take the offer if it was presented as one he couldn't refuse.

## TWO
## INSIST THE ELECTION WAS STOLEN
## AND REFUSE TO LEAVE

If Trump ends up winning the Electoral College, or if it's thrown to the House, the president should immediately declare that the election was rigged. Stolen. Then refuse to leave office. Send the military to seize voting machines. Unleash a barrage of lawsuits, and in the meantime simply remain in power. Mimic the over-60 lawsuits Trump pulled in 2020. Drag it out. Refuse to leave until they are all settled. If a decision goes against you, appeal. Insist there's proof of the stolen election. Get your supporters to rally in D.C. Use the power of the office while you've got the power of the office. Then pack the fuck out of the Court. They already stole the court. Steal it back. Then stall it out. And refuse to leave. Let Republicans scream their heads off. They already are. Who cares?

Then, once the histrionics have subsided, Biden could make a speech from the Oval Office, and accuse Trump of rigging the election. "My fellow Americans. My opponent made the claim in 2020 that the election was rigged and even went so far as to send his supporters to attack Congress and impede the vote certification. However in this election, he did, in fact, rig it in an attempt to seize power, which would have, in effect, brought down our democracy. It didn't work out that way but we need to restore faith in our democratic process. Therefore, I am declaring this election null and void. I will remain in power until such time as we can have a legitimate election, one in which Donald Trump watches from the TV lounge in a Federal Penitentiary or the McDonald's in the Moscow airport. Meanwhile, I am also expanding the Supreme Court and installing both Bill and Hillary Clinton as judges, declaring that all women have the right to an abortion, and the Electoral College null and void. All future elections will be decided by the popular vote. And if Republicans don't like it they can suck it.

## THREE
## STEAL THE ELECTION

This may be somewhat of a modest proposal but it's the one I like best: DEMOCRATS SHOULD STEAL THE ELECTION FOR KAMALA HARRIS. That's right. Actually steal it. Do everything Trump accused Democrats of doing. Rig the voting machines. Screw with the vote count. Throw out Republican ballots. Stop Republicans from voting in person. No water. No food. Long lines. Make them wait for hours. Then, when they get to the front, tell them they're not registered to vote. Collude with Secretaries of State and Governors to pre-rig the count. Send your own electors from every state in the nation. This time the Vice President would definitely certify them, ironically declaring herself the winner. Who cares how much screaming they do. Who's going to stop it? All they can do is yell. And sue. So what. Stall them in the courts. Meanwhile, Kamala Harris is inaugurated in January. Last time the Democrats weren't in power so it was really impossible for them to actually steal it. This time, it might not be.

Then, just for flavor, tell Trump privately that it was stolen. Imagine the fat Orange psychopath crying wolf, screaming to Fox while and firing off furious blasts on Truth Social about the election being "stollen," but only this time it would actually have been stolen but no one would believe him.

Let him run around the country, screaming. Take boozy Rudy along for the ride, assuming he can stand up straight. Return to Four Seasons Total Landscaping. It would be the boy who cried wolf. He's already done this bit. His people might even get bored with the routine. He could call for violence but this time no one would be willing to storm the Capitol and risk prison. Imagine the irony of screwing him with his own shit. Even his own people will start to roll their eyes as he melted down.

Steve Bannon's enlarged heart would explode. Steven

Miller would be so frozen in shock he'd remain in place until daybreak and a shard of sunlight would blast him into vampire dust. The Trump kids would sell him out in a second once they see him melt down. They'd stick him in a home. Melania will be long gone.

The irony would be perfect. He'd scream his fucking head off and this time he'd be right but people would be so jaded with this shit that they'd assume he was just being a sore loser, Even if his trained paramilitary monkeys descended on DC, the president could use the Insurrection Act and deploy the National Guard and the military, and quash the rebellion.

Perhaps the ultimate irony would be that it would infuriate Trump to the point that he'd flip out. Blow his wig off. Shoot Adderall snot rockets out of his nose as he shit himself. Maybe in public. During a rally. Or while in court. Or outside on the courtroom steps. With cameras rolling. Now that would be great TV! HUGE! THE GREATEST SHOW EVER! RATINGS LIKE NO ONE'S EVER SEEN BEFORE! THE GREATEST RATINGS IN THE HISTORY OF THE WORLD!!
It could work.  It would also put the country back on track and put future elections out of steal-able range.

Of course, there's the matter of whether the military would back up the play. They could stage a coup of their own, take over the White House and usher Trump into power. Because, at that point, the question becomes: What is power? And the answer is: power goes to the people with the most guns. Which it actually is, anyway. The social contract, democratic government, and the rule of law has been our safeguard against that reality.

## CONCLUSION

I have been writing this book for three years. I've tried to keep it up to date, incorporating recent events, both ordinary and game-changers. The first Biden debate was shocking enough. Until Trump got shot at. And a guy got killed. And two people got wounded. And the shooter was killed. One takeaway from that event: Like football, history seems to be a game of inches.

I am struggling with putting that event into perspective. I can't get all the way to empathy, given the hatred and violence this guy has fomented over the last fifteen years. American life has been shaped by assassinations and attempted assassinations. But it's not supposed to be the way we do things here. My empathy goes to the local guy who was murdered. And to the people who were wounded. Even to the twisted loner who grabbed his daddy's gun and tried to blast his way into history. It's all one great big American tragedy.

Meanwhile, we're still left with questions. How did he make it to that building rooftop? With a line of sight. Unseen by any Secret Service, or security. How long did he plan it? How did he know where to go? And why was there no hospital press conference with doctors detailing the extent of the injury and his treatment. This is Lee Harvey Oswald Book Depository shit. Social media is already rife with conspiracy theories. As well as people opining about Trump's sick jokes about Nancy Pelosi's husband getting attacked.

He's such a twisted person that people's minds went right to "staged." "Fake." That's as much a testament to who he is as well as who we've become. He played the martyr card right through the RNC convention by wearing a Maxi Pad Scotch taped to his ear. He probably figured the pity vote would attract moderates in swing states.

Then, to top that off, Biden pulled out of the race. And Kamala Harris is the nominee, The Democratic party has been re-energized as we head toward the convention in, of all places, Chicago, as people speculate on who she will pick as a running mate. Hopefully it will be someone who can add even more power to the ticket, while branding Trump as the one who is old and out of touch. The contenders seem to be Josh Shapiro, Mark Kelly, Roy Cooper, and Andy Beshear. They could go for Adam Kinzinger. Switch it up. Go bi-partisan. Outflank the motherfuckers. Pick off disaffected Republicans. It won't happen. But it's a thought. I'm leaning toward Shapiro because he's tough, smart, a fighter and, well, Pennsylvania. But also in the running is Minnesota Governor, Tim Walz. He's got a solid, middle-America vibe and a tough, but inviting way of speaking. He could pull in rust belt men and provide a strong counterbalance to the ticket. The picture of Walz and Harris could work.

Biden's withdrawal and Harris' nomination seem to have recalibrated the race. There's even speculation that Trump could dump Vance and choose someone to balance the ticket. And also because Vance is coming off creepy with his "childless cat lady" crack. He's completely transparent in his efforts to try to say the meanest shit he can think of. He's like Trump's Mini-Mean. I wouldn't be shocked if they waited until after the DNC convention, told Vance to pull out, then put in Nikki Haley. I know she'd take it, as she's the most craven, nakedly ambitious politician I've seen in years. In GOP minds, it might neutralize some of Harris' appeal.

Another aspect of the race is that Democrats are energized. Confident. Young people are registering to vote. Donations are pouring in. But as pundits analyze the difference between Harris' previous presidential campaign in 2020 and this one, it's important to remember that it's not just the candidate, it's the times. In 2020, she was just another Democrat, trying to find a lane in a crowded field. This time, the winds of history are at her back. There is an importance to her candidacy that wasn't there before.

Emotionally, I am stuck somewhere between 2008 Obama "Yes, we can" power and optimism, and 2016 "I'm with Her" sense of self-righteousness, but with a looming undercurrent of impending doom.

We need a champion to take the fight to Trump, not just with facts and stats, but with sticks and stones. I know there is renewed enthusiasm in the party. People are networking, organizing, raising money, getting ready to make phone calls and knock on doors. And all that is important. But Kamala Harris need to take Trump down in public. Even though he will most likely punk out of a debate, she needs to start carving him up and neutralizing his power. Because after all this time, and all his crimes, and all his clowning, and declarations of his intention to become a dictator, he shouldn't be a thing. American should have expelled him from our system like a Taco Bell burrito. But the polls are way too close. He could return to power. And, as I've written many times, that's not on him; that's on us.

As we race toward November we are still one country, living in two separate realities. A radical theocratic minority has become emboldened, going all in on the Heritage Foundation's Project 2025 – a blueprint for totalitarian, theocratic life in America. It's the culture wars turned up to eleven with the Supreme Court putting their hand on the scale. Trump's working from the same playbook. Heads I win; tales it's rigged. This is not going to go down peacefully.

Forget what we all saw play out in public on January 6th and in the months and days leading up to it. Taking the bank robbery analogy from before, they've declared that no one can prove robbery, and if it turned out that Trump robbed the bank it was in his official capacity and he had the right to rob the bank and, therefore, can't be prosecuted. Not only that, but if he's elected bank president again he can gut the whole system install his flunkies at every level and take revenge on his enemies. This is not histrionics. This is his stated intent.

This is the fourth book I have written on this phenomenon. I ended all three on cliffhangers because I had no idea what was coming next and, besides, I was tired of writing and it seemed more dramatic to stop and imagine what the future would bring.

In *Welcome to Dumbfuckistan* (2016) I wrote: "We assume Orwell's 1984 dystopian nightmare can't happen here, yet we've been narcotized into a more ominous Orwellian somnambulism. We're inebriated on our own mythology, priapic at our military supremacy and malleable via our iconic imagery, whether it's Jesus or the flag. Jacked up on Adderall, Red Bull and patriotism we only unite in war, tragedy and the Super Bowl. We've become style over substance, image over reality, propaganda over truth and symbol over meaning. Perhaps evolution is a myth in that we seem to be devolving. The Roman Empire collapsed due to war, overexpansion and corruption. The British Empire dissolved due to cultural arrogance and imperialistic hubris. Sadly, as we devolve from Democracy to Idiocracy America may become the first world power to crumble under the weight of its own stupidity."

Ok, that didn't happen but it was an accurate description of a phenomenon that was occurring in the country at the time, and is continuing to play out.

In a second book, *Freak-Out* (2017), which was a post-mortem on the 2016 election, I wrote: "It's a sad fact of life that human beings are susceptible to the impulses of a dictator. When economic desperation, anger, and changing times conspire, people don't think rationally, they react emotionally. This can open the door for tyrants who find convenient scapegoats for our problems and promise easy solutions. By reducing the complexities of life to simple categories, they take advantage of people's frustrations and use them as a steppingstone to power." I left off wondering about life as an expat.

In the third book, *Death to America*, which came out a few months before the 2020 election, I wrote: "There's a good chance we'll survive Trump. And while all the references to dictatorships and the Trumpocalypse may seem like hysterical overreactions, I'd rather overreact and be relieved than assume the best and be shocked."

One thing is for sure: On Election Day, one group of Democrats on social media is going to tell another group of

Democrats on social media: "I told you so."

I would like to be more sanguine about this election but I got an upfront look at what the country could turn into. Back in 2020, I saw a 100-truck MAGA caravan lumber down the main street in my neighborhood. People were blaring their horns, and waving their flags. And while I got an eerie tingle of what my ancestors might have felt living in Germany during the rise of the Nazis, they never turned down my block. I assuaged my fear with the assumption that they were just goose-stepping fools, flexing, yelling, waving flags, and honking horns. It was all for show. Yet, it could be a matter of time before they're grabbing their guns, jumping off trucks, and filtering through the neighborhood on a Jew hunt. It wouldn't take much to get them there. They will follow orders, however direct or implied. As much as I dislike the idea of owning a gun, I am almost ready to get one just in case. I really don't think it will happen. Then again, neither did my ancestors.

I could spend the rest of this year writing, re-writing, thinking, watching, and editing, but I can't. After three years, I have to get this out and go back to screaming at my TV. There will be mistakes. Repetition. Typos. I will leave off before the DNC convention.

I knew late last year that 2024 was going to hit full chaos. That we didn't yet know what we didn't know. That the heat was going to get turned way up.

The only thing I do know is that anything could happen. A rogue attack somewhere in the world on the scale of 9/11. They did the unthinkable. We humans are capable of it. Self-destruction may be in our DNA. Life may want to live but we still seem hell-bent on self-annihilation. With all the fascination about AI and other technological advancements, one might think we'd use that intelligence to improve life on the planet. Build farms, schools, figure out clean energy, take guns out of the hands of murderers, and turn them into plowshares. But we don't, either because we can't or we just don't want to. Instead we make more guns and bombs and spread them around the world. We will, literally, be the death of us. Meanwhile, I am trying not to panic although I am thinking of putting a go-bag together.

Democracy is a gift on how to live the good life. But it's only as valid as the hands in which it's been placed at any given time. Right now it's at risk of being molested out of all recognition. We haven't evolved into higher beings with higher consciousness just because we made some social progress over the previous centuries. Not everyone was along for the ride. Some hated the changes and nursed their anger in relative silence, waiting for a chance to strike back. Trump was their revenge.

Politicians love to pander about the fundamental goodness of the American people. Bullshit. We're as evil as anyone else. We just had better guardrails on our selfish behavior. Better systems in place to rein us in. But they didn't make us better people. We're not a society. We're Jurassic Park with fences that held up. Up to now.

I used to think that even though we've had our aberrations over the years -- clowns, grifters, egomaniacs, powermongers, people who seized the national attention or preyed on public fear, sentiments, or anger, and resentment and rode it to power -- that the American system was resilient. It would bend but never break. That the lunatic fringe could never take over. That it can't happen here. Wrong. It can happen here. Whether it does happen is still in the air. The title of this book stated that America was too dumb for democracy. That's not the totality. Maybe the title should have been:

AMERICA

TOO
GOOD
FOR
FASCISM

TOO
DUMB
ANGRY
RACIST
SEXIST
SEXUALLY REPRESSED
HOMOPHOBIC
THEOCRATIC
SELF-LOATHING
INSECURE
SCARED
GREEDY
CROOKED
POWER HUNGRY
BRAINWASHED
AND
VIOLENT

FOR
DEMOCRACY

Ok, that may be harsh. And maybe at times I've been too harsh as I try to comprehend the phenomenon of my country falling apart at the seams. Maybe instead of criticizing people on the other side, I should have been trying to understand them. Maybe even find common ground. Fighting back when I should be reaching out. Maybe I haven't been compassionate. Maybe I've been too mean, cruel, sarcastic, arrogant, smart-ass, and insulting. Maybe I've been judgmental, and elitist in criticizing his people, not appreciating that some are going through a tough time and looking for answers even if momentarily choosing the wrong one. Or maybe they're afraid of change, or grappling with their inner demons, but they don't want to destroy the system and descend into dictatorship. Maybe they just want to feel heard. Maybe I've missed a basic truth -- that the American people are fundamentally good, honest, decent, and patriotic. Fine. Prove me wrong.

# AFTERWORD

Should anyone want to engage, I'm on X/Twitter. Bots and assholes will be blocked.

TRUMP
FOR
PRISON!

HARRIS
FOR
PRESIDENT!

# BIOGRAPHY

I am a native New Yorker who has lived in Los Angeles for 30 years, working as a TV writer/producer/director. I've produced over 300 TV episodes, on shows such as *Wings*, *Becker*, and *The Exes*. I also wrote and directed an independent feature -- *L.A. Blues*.

In addition to working in television I've written about politics and culture for *The Huffington Post* and *attn.com*, and published articles in the *L.A. Times* and *Creative Screenwriting*.

I've written seven books, including: *Hello, Lied the Agent*, (2006) a behind-the-scenes look at TV development; *Deconstructing God*, (2010), *Welcome to Dumbfuckistan* (2016), *Freak-Out* (2017), and *Death to America.* (2020). I also published a book of drawings entitled, *Talking Heads*.

www.ingramcontent.com/pod-product-compliance
Lightning Source LLC
Chambersburg PA
CBHW061039250726
48653CB00001B/162